LEGAL ISSUES FOR INDUSTRIAL EDUCATORS

LEGAL ISSUES FOR INDUSTRIAL EDUCATORS

**FORREST GATHERCOAL
AND
SAM STERN**

PRAKKEN PUBLICATIONS, INC.

Library of Congress Catalog Card No. 86-60598
ISBN: 0-911168-64-8 (hardcover)
      0-911168-65-6 (paperback)

Contents

CONTENTS

LEGAL ISSUES
FOR
INDUSTRIAL
EDUCATORS

Preface

This book is intended for all those who are concerned about legal issues related to industrial education. While these issues are of primary interest to industrial educators—including industrial arts/technology education, trade and industrial, and technical education teachers of all grade levels—they also concern other professionals who share responsibility for assuring that industrial education classes meet their legal, as well as educational, obligations. These individuals include administrators, advisory-committee members, risk managers, insurance representatives, and attorneys who work with educational programs. This book is also appropriate as a basic or supplementary text for both preservice and in-service industrial education courses in colleges or universities.

Whether in a middle school technology education class or a community college advanced machining course, industrial education teachers continually find themselves challenged to make difficult and critical decisions related to students, colleagues, equipment, and money. The purpose of this book is to help them develop a basis for decision making based on sound legal and ethical considerations.

During the past three decades, lawmakers have reshaped a great deal of our educational law and policy. While many educators have some awareness of the increasing amount of litigation and legislation related to education, most do not understand how the new laws and policies relate to their areas of responsibility. As a result, they are uncertain and uncomfortable about the legality of many routine decisions they make in the course of a typical day. The increasing level of legislation and policy-making is of particular interest to industrial educators who deal with such issues as safety and liability, cooperative work experience, insurance, preparing recommendations, sex discrimination, handicapped and disadvantaged students, formulating rules, and due process. Each chapter in this book addresses a critical legal issue from the industrial educator's perspective. The book's primary purpose is to alert industrial educators to relevant legal background and provide guidelines for decision making related to each issue. We have made every effort to eliminate as much legal terminology as possible and still communicate important legal concepts. Chapters include case citations, references, and resources for those interested in additional information and materials.

In some sections, it may appear to the reader that we provide contradictory information or suggestions. Such contradictions and ambiguities reflect the nature of the law. Cases are decided on specific facts and arguments presented to the courts by opposing counsel. What appears as different treatment in the courts for similar actions may arise from such factors as varying details of procedure followed in the particular situations involved, differing institutional settings, or differing legal bases used for courtroom arguments. Each chapter emphasizes the importance of industrial educators basing their decisions on clearly defined and enunciated educational objectives. Rarely will any basis other than the educational objectives and the mission of a school, be it a middle school or a technical college, suffice as legal grounds for administrative actions.

Some readers may question how much law an educator must know and whether or not the professional fields of law and education need to be considered in relation to each other. The saying "a little knowledge is a dangerous thing" is an axiom in both law and education. As the material in this book demonstrates, given the current environment, almost every educational issue or administrative act has legal implications of one type or another. Failing to be aware of these implications may lead to serious problems, unnecessary risk to teachers and students, loss of valuable time, and significant financial expense. Our intent is not to scare industrial educators who are concerned about legal issues, but instead to empower them with information that will help them make critical decisions on a sound legal and educational basis.

This book would not have been possible without the contributions of many people. We are indebted to our wives, Joan and Kitzie, who provided valuable support to this project and our professional careers. We are especially thankful for the support of the people at

Prakken Publications, who care deeply about industrial education: Larry Prakken, president of Prakken Publications and longtime advocate for industrial education, who encouraged us to pursue this project; Alan Jones, publisher and executive editor of Prakken Publications, who supported and nurtured this project from the beginning; and Susanne Peckham, editorial director and senior editor of Prakken's SCHOOL SHOP magazine, for her careful and skilled editing.

The following individuals read portions of the manuscript and offered valuable comments and suggestions: David Bjorkquist of the University of Minnesota; Rupert Evans and Jacob Stern of the University of Illinois; Roger Haskell of the University of Tennessee; Merle Strong, of the University of Wisconsin; Kenneth Keudall of the Oregon Builders Board; William Lilly, Rodger Shoemaker, and Gil Hodges of Fred S. James Insurance; Jerry Olson of the Pennsylvania Department of Education; William Prakken, a practicing attorney; Kendall Starkweather of the International Technology Education Association; Robert Barr; Warren Suzuki, Bonnie Young, Marie Egbert, Jay Conroy, and Stephanie Sanford of Oregon State University; and Frederick Welch of Pennsylvania State University; and Glen Otto, Oregon state senator. Final responsibility for all of the material presented in this book rests with the authors.

Finally, we express our appreciation to our students and the industrial educators who have participated in our workshops. They motivated us to write this book and challenged us to identify and clarify legal issues that impact industrial education.

CHAPTER 1
Safety and Liability

A junior high technology education teacher stands at her class-room door watching and talking to students in the hallway as they walk to their last-period class. A few students edge past her into the shop, talking and carrying on, as most students will before class starts. Moments later, she hears a scream, followed by sobbing, from one of the girls in the class. The teacher rushes into the room and over to a girl, who holds a hand over her left eye. Several classmates are trying to comfort her while one boy apologizes for accidentally poking her eye with the end of a piece of sheet metal. The teacher helps the girl to the school nurse, who, after a quick look at her eye, rushes the girl to the hospital emergency room. Later that evening the teacher receives a call informing her that the girl has lost the sight in her left eye, with no hope for recovery. The teacher is also informed that the girl's parents may bring suit against the teacher and the school district for negligent supervision of the classroom.

This is a tragic accident, and one that can happen very suddenly in any industrial education teacher's classroom. If it happened in your class, would you be legally prepared? What legal action could the student's parents take against you and the school district? What legal defenses are available? Will you have to pay for your defense attorney? For a possible judgment against you? What steps could you have taken to prevent the accident?

Industrial education teachers encounter many challenges every teaching day. Not only must they face a rapidly changing content and the management of equipment and facilities, but they must also maintain a safe work environment for themselves and their students. Industrial education classes offer students the opportunity to learn the correct and safe operation of tools and equipment. They provide many students' first exposure to the use of power tools and equipment. The safety habits these students learn in their industrial education classes can help them throughout their lives.

As an industrial education teacher, one of your primary concerns must be the safety and welfare of your students. But, regardless of how safe you make your program, how carefully you give instructions and supervise your classes, accidents can and will happen. This chapter provides an overview of the legal process following an accident and presents a set of guidelines you can follow to help prevent accidents in your industrial education classes and to protect yourself, your program, and your school district from liability.

Tort Liability

A parent or student taking you to court will file a civil action in tort. The word *tort* derives from the Latin *tortus*, meaning twisted. In personal relationships, the term *twisted* applies to an activity that in some way deviates from a normally acceptable pattern of behavior. The socially and legally acceptable relationship between two persons may be breached when, by either an act or a failure to act, one party causes injury to the other.

The term *tort* may further be defined as a group of civil wrongs for which a court will provide a remedy in the form of damages. Tort actions are brought by individuals to compensate for harm caused by the unreasonable conduct of others. Social norms and customs provide the basis for legal proceedings in determining what is considered unacceptable or unreasonable conduct.

A civil action for tort is initiated and maintained by the injured party to obtain compensation for the injury suffered, as opposed to a criminal proceeding where the action is brought by the state to protect the public from actions of a wrongdoer. In a criminal prosecution, the state prosecutes not to compensate the injured person, but to protect the public from further wrongful acts. Since criminal law does not and was never intended to compensate an injured individual, social justice demanded the introduction of the action in tort.

Grounds for action in tort can be divided into three categories: (1) negligence, (2) strict liability, and (3) intentional interference with an individual.

Negligence

Negligence holds by far the greatest potential as grounds for action involving accidents that occur in industrial education classes. The legal definition states that a person is *negligent* when, without intending any wrong, he or she commits an act or fails to act to prevent an occurrence that *under the circumstances an ordinary prudent person ought reasonably to foresee* will expose another person to unreasonable risk of harm. In determining whether conduct will subject another to an unreasonable risk of harm, a person must consider the surrounding circumstances that a reasonably prudent person would consider, possess the knowledge an ordinary reasonable person would possess, and use the judgment and discretion a person of reasonable intelligence would use under the same or similar circumstances. To find someone negligent, the plaintiff must allege and prove

1. A *duty* on the part of the actor to protect others against unreasonable risks.

2. A failure on the part of the actor to exercise a *standard of care* commensurate with the risks involved.

3. That the conduct of the actor is the *proximate cause* or *legal cause* of the injury—in other words, a causal connection must exist between the act and the resulting injury.

4. That *injury, actual loss, or damage* result from the act.

The first step in applying the legal concept of negligence to the industrial education classroom involves determining whether or not the teacher has a *duty* to protect the students in his or her class from unreasonable risk. In most situations, it is relatively easy to determine that a duty exists since students are assigned to a class and are under the industrial education teacher's supervision. In other situations, an industrial education teacher's duty may prove more difficult to establish. Consider situations where your assistant principal works in the shop late at night making wooden toys for her children or some of your students use school tools to work on their cars in the school parking lot after school hours. In either of these situations, would you have a *duty*? For negligence to exist, a legal duty must be formed between the teacher and the injured person.

The second element involves the question of a *standard of care* commensurate with the risks involved. The usual legal test applied to this standard considers whether or not the teacher's performance reflects what a reasonably prudent industrial education teacher would have foreseen and provided for under the same or similar circumstances. If the teacher's behavior falls below this standard of care, the second element of negligence is fulfilled. However, if the standard of care is met or surpassed, the industrial education teacher would not be considered negligent. This begs the question of how society determines what standard of care is commensurate with the risks involved in an educational activity. It constitutes a question of fact for the jury to decide and is ordinarily based on expert testimony from professionals in the field.

If the case in question involves a welding accident, the student's attorney would call in other welding teachers and authenticated experts in the field to testify to the quality of instruction and facilities involved in the student's injury. At the completion of the student's evidence to the jury intended to show that the teacher had fallen below the standard of care normally exercised by professionals in the field of welding, the instructor would begin his or her parade of experts and evidence showing that the school had adequate facilities and that the instructor gave proper instructions and took proper safety precautions, and therefore did meet the standard of care required. Cross-examination by the opposing attorney tests the expertise of the experts and brings out inconsistencies in testimony. The jury weighs all the testimony, the facts of the incident, and the evidence presented by the experts in its deliberations. It then rules as a question of fact whether the teacher's performance was consistent with what a reasonably prudent industrial educator would have foreseen and provided for under the same or similar circumstances.

The third element in the determination of negligence is the *proximate* or *legal cause* of the injury, which necessitates a causal connection between the teacher's act and the student's resulting injury. In other worlds, this element considers whether the teacher's falling below the profession's standard of care was the cause of or reason for the *injury, loss, or damage,* the fourth and last element.

All four elements must be alleged and proved to hold the teacher liable for the student's injury. If one of the four elements is not proved, the student has no cause of action. Here is a brief summary of grounds for negligence: If an industrial educator has a legal duty to protect the student, fails to meet the standard of a reasonable industrial education professional, and in so doing causes an injury to the student, the jury must find the teacher negligent.

Although all of these elements are important, most tort liability cases depend on whether the teacher did or did not meet the standard of care acceptable to other professionals in the same field. To protect yourself, read your professional journals, attend professional meetings and workshops, and try to keep up with new developments related to your field and safety. If one of your students is injured, the courts will make a judgment based on current professional industrial education standards.

Defenses against Negligence Claims

Contributory and comparative negligence is conduct on the part of the plaintiff that falls below the standard to which the plaintiff should conform for his or her own protection. It involves a legally contributing cause that cooperates with the negligence of the defendant to bring about the plaintiff's harm. This is the "I told you so" defense, and it is the defense used most often by teachers in dealing with a lawsuit. In most injury cases, the student has foolishly or carelessly gone ahead with something he or she was instructed not to do and receives an injury as a result of that action. If the jury believes that the student negligently contributed to his or her own injury, the court holds for the teacher and the student usually does not receive a monetary award. This is a very harsh outcome for a student who may have been just a little careless in a situation where the school is mainly at fault.

In pursuit of greater fairness, most states have through legislation adopted a more reasonable law called *comparative negligence.* Comparative negligence allows juries to find the degree to which each party is negligent, and it authorizes recovery based on the relative degree of fault. For example, a student who was only slightly careless might be found 25 percent negligent, resulting in the school district paying 75 percent of the damages. This legal principle is important enough that industrial education teachers should investigate their respective state laws on comparative negligence to determine how a court in their state would instruct a jury.

Assumption of risk is the defense used against a plaintiff who has adequate knowledge of the danger involved, voluntarily enters into a relationship with the defendant, and, by so doing, agrees to take his or her own chances. Essential to this defense is the point that the plaintiff fully understands and has complete knowledge of the risks involved in the activity. This defense has close ties to contributory negligence, but where contributory negligence relies more on careless behavior, assumption of risk addresses the adventurous nature of the student's action. An experienced industrial education student working in a shop area with power equipment provides a good example of someone who, based on past experience, fully understands the hazardous nature of the equipment and the presence of some danger just being in the room and working with power tools. Assumption of risk applies because the experienced student voluntarily enters the shop activity knowing full well that risks exist. Assumption of risk will not usually protect an industrial education teacher from being found negligent if the teacher in fact fell below the standard of care. However, it does offer viable defense for some types of injuries and could mitigate damages against the school in case of teacher negligence. Although many states have subsumed assumption within comparative negligence, understanding its legal applications can help teachers in their promulgation of class rules and instructions.

Immunity is the defense generally conferred on: (1) national and state governments, unless abrogated by statute; (2) public officials performing judicial, quasi-judicial, or discretionary functions; (3) charitable organizations granted immunity in some states; (4) infants, under certain conditions; and (5) in some cases, insane persons. States that grant immunity simply do not allow government employees to be held liable in tort when they act within the scope of their employment. However, because of public resentment against governmental agencies not being held responsible for damages caused by their operation, most states have enacted legislation that allows holding governmental agencies liable for damages they incur. The laws involved modify the old common law principle that "the king can do no wrong." States vary on granting immunity, so it is important to inquire about the laws in your state.

Unavoidable and nonforeseeable accident is an applicable defense if an injury is not caused by negligence, as legally defined, but results from an accident in which no one holds legal responsibility. This is sometimes referred to as the "act of God" defense. Consider, for example, a situation where an instructor has students performing construction work on a house. A rare, sudden flood occurs—a

"100-year" flood, in the terms of a classic legal hypothetical example. The flood waters weaken the building's foundation and the house collapses, causing injury to a student working on the roof. In this situation, the instructor could formulate an effective defense by saying that the injury could not be foreseen by a reasonably prudent teacher under the same circumstances. On the other hand, if a good possibility of flooding in the area had been predicted, a jury would not allow such a defense. This type of defense is not often used, but in appropriate circumstances it presents a very understandable argument for nonliability.

Intervening act or event is a defense used in a case where, even though the teacher is negligent, the negligence is not the proximate cause of the injury. The real cause of the injury arises from an intervening act or event which often results from the conduct of a third party. For example, a student new to the metalshop who lacks proper instruction injures himself while working on a drill press. If these were the only facts, the instructor would probably be found negligent for not giving the student proper instructions. However, if the evidence also shows that another student intentionally pushed the injured student, out of revenge for an earlier fight, causing his hand to move into the path of the drill bit, the second student's intervening act would allow the jury to find the teacher's failure to give instructions *not* the proximate cause of the injury. This defense relieves the teacher of legal liability for the injury. It is used as a response to the third element of an action of negligence, proximate cause, and can prove very effective if other students are involved in an incident.

Strict Liability

Strict liability, the second ground for actions in tort, occurs when a teacher's activity involves abnormal danger to others. Both intentional interference and negligence are based on the supposition that someone was injured at the fault of another party. Damage awards based on strict liability arise where a person has been injured through no one's fault. The court reasons that strict responsibility lies with those who, even with proper care, expose the community to the risk of something very dangerous.

Consider the situation where the United States' first space station lost power while circling the earth and was going to fall. This provides a good example of a situation where someone might be hurt, but at the fault of no one. In this case, in the unlikely event that the space station's fall had injured someone, the United States government would have been strictly liable and would have paid all damages incurred without question of fault. The same would hold true for an industrial education teacher who allowed students to use a power saw without the required safety guard.

The hazards in schools created by normal industrial education activity, gym equipment, laboratory experiments, or field trips present possibilities of actions that involve strict liability. Although strict liability is not a common ground for actions involving industrial educators, it is far more prevalent than the third and final ground for action in tort, intentional interference.

Intentional Interference

Intentional interference, sometimes called malfeasance, is an intentional act by a person that results in injury to another. Intent exists when someone realizes with substantial certainty that his or her act will create a specific result that is likely to cause injury. The best-known examples of intentional torts are assault, battery, interference with peace of mind, false imprisonment, libel, and slander. The tort of intentional interference seldom arises in a school setting. To be guilty of intentional interference, a teacher would have to act with the sole purpose of hurting someone or in a grossly wanton manner.

Teacher Protection against Lawsuits

Many industrial education teachers understandably show concern about student injuries and the resulting possibility of monetary judgment against them and their families that could cause personal financial loss. Legislation passed in many states protects public school teachers from personal financial responsibility for injuries that occur in their classrooms. These laws are commonly referred to as *save-harmless* statutes. They require a school district to defend, save harmless, and indemnify any of its officers or employees against any tort claim or demand that arises from an alleged act or omission that occurs during performance of duty. Under these laws, school districts must not only provide legal representation for the teacher's defense but must also pay the cost of judgments rendered against the teacher. Several requirements, however, must be filled for the teacher to benefit from this protection and from the coverage provided the teacher by other insurance policies.

First, the teacher must be working within the scope of his or her employment. Teachers not functioning within their scope of employment, are legally considered "on a frolic of their own" and leave themselves wide open to personal liability. If, for example, you are an automotive teacher who occasionally allows students to use your home garage to repair their cars with tools from the school lab, do you act within the scope of your employment or are you "on a frolic of your own?" One good test to determine your position regarding scope of employment asks whether your administrator or immediate supervisor knows what you are doing and has given either express or tacit approval of the activity. If you feel uncertain about the propriety of your planned actions or activities, an authorization from your administrator may save you a lot of time and money.

A second thing to keep in mind is that your insurance and state statutes do not protect you from acts of malfeasance or willful or wanton neglect of duty. Malfeasance involves an intentional wrong designed to hurt someone. Willful or wanton neglect of duty is the reckless disregard of the rights of others or arises where injury is likely the result of a wrongful act. For example, willful and wanton behavior occurs when an intoxicated teacher has an accident while driving students home from a field trip.

The Minnesota Supreme Court decided a complex case on this issue involving a teacher who was alleged to have had sexual contact with a 16-year-old high school girl. The appeal involved the girl, her parents, the teacher, the school district, the state teachers' association's liability insurance company, and the school district's liability insurance company.[1] As a result of the teacher's contact with the girl, her psychological health deteriorated and she entered the hospital on numerous occasions because of suicidal tendencies, depression, and anorexia. Her medical expenses totaled approximately $90,000.

The Minnesota Supreme Court held that (1) the Horace Mann insurance policy carried by the teachers' association excluded coverage for defense costs and indemnity of the teacher; (2) the Security

Insurance Company (homeowner's policy carried by the teacher) was likewise not liable; (3) the Fireman's Fund Insurance Company (liability insurance carried by the school district) was also not liable; and (4) the school district was held to the duty of defending the teacher under the provisions of the Minnesota Code but had no obligation to indemnify against judgments or settlements if malfeasance or willful or wanton neglect of duty were.found to exist.

The two examples of egregious behavior described above clearly would not bring the teacher within the protection of personal or association insurance coverage or of the state's save-harmless statute. Inquire about the language in your insurance policies and the state laws governing your financial protection as a teacher. Far more cases are settled out of court by insurance companies than through the court process. For more information on insurance coverage and how it relates to industrial education programs and teachers, refer to Chapter 4.

Representing the School

If a lawsuit for negligence is brought against your school district, community college, or technical school, the complaint will probably name the teacher, department chair or immediate supervisor, the principal or dean of instruction, the superintendent, and the school board, as well as equipment and machinery manufacturers and others who may have had some direct or indirect responsibility for a student's injury. When the school receives the complaint, it calls in the school district's attorney, who will usually assume leadership for planning and representing the defense of the case. Because you, as the teacher, were the person directly responsible for classroom supervision at the time of the injury, the school attorney will direct most attention at you and the incidents leading to and immediately following the accident. As regretful as you feel about the student's injury, you must now focus your attention on the job at hand and do everything possible to help the school attorney present a good defense.

It is helpful after a serious accident to document as soon as possible the events surrounding the incident. Make note of instructions you had given the injured student, what you were doing when the injury occurred, room conditions at the time, statements or admissions by the injured student or bystanders, and any other factors that could help set up one or more of the legal defenses presented earlier in this chapter. Photographs of the accident scene should be taken as soon as possible to help accurately describe the accident. Memory tends to diminish with time. Accurate and well-organized notes can help you prepare to appear in court before a jury and hold up well on cross-examination by the other side's attorney. Consistent use of accident reports can help you and your attorney be prepared for a legal or insurance case.

When working with an attorney representing the school district, it is very important that you be completely open and honest about all facts and circumstances surrounding the case. Something you consider unimportant could have great legal significance and prove crucial to a good defense. Do not try to hide facts to "get off the hook" or "make yourself look good." Complete and accurate information from you could lead to an early out-of-court settlement with a fair amount of insurance money going to the injured student. Suppressing facts often leads to surprises at the trial for your attorney and to the possibility that he or she will be caught unprepared to meet the legal issues raised by the other side. Be accurate and honest with information for your attorney. Remember that attorneys do not like surprises.

The Other Attorney

It is equally important to remember that the attorney for the other side also wants to know what your testimony will be. Like the school attorney, he or she will focus on you because of your proximity to and participation in the events surrounding the incident. You must consult the school attorney as to what information you should divulge about the case to the attorney or investigators representing the injured student. Most attorneys recommend that their clients talk to the other attorney only in their presence. The legal system allows the other attorney to request a deposition to gather information about the case. To take a deposition, you will be called to the courthouse or an attorney's office to answer questions about the case posed by the other attorney. Your answers, given under oath, will usually be recorded by a court reporter or with a tape recorder. The deposition will be taken in the presense of your school attorney who can advise and assist you in your responses and object to irrelevant and leading questions posed by the other attorney.

Have the facts of the incident clearly in mind before beginning the deposition. Be open and honest with your answers because the testimony you give under oath at a deposition must be the same as the testimony you will give if the case goes to trial. Do not volunteer information and answer only the questions asked. If the school has a good defense and you present yourself and the facts well at the deposition, the case is likely to be settled between the attorneys in a fair and equitable manner, making a jury trial unnecessary. This can save considerable time and money as well as avoid the pressures and frustrations connected with a lengthy court trial. A teacher involved in a lawsuit should play it "close to the vest" and make every effort to consult the school attorney before taking part in any investigation or talking to the attorney for the other side.

Guidelines to Prevent Accidents

Should your case be one of the few that goes to trial, your school attorney must present evidence to the jury that clearly shows you saw and did everything before and after the accident that a reasonable and prudent teacher would have foreseen and done under the same or similar circumstances. This raises two questions: What things should an industrial education teacher do and provide for to prevent injuries? How are the steps taken by a teacher used to assist the school attorney in the defense of a possible lawsuit if an injury should occur?

Courts will hold a reasonable and prudent teacher accountable for four basic guidelines in meeting the standard of care expected by the profession. Although an accident may happen even if a teacher observes these four guidelines, sufficiently addressing them will in most cases legally remove the teacher as the proximate cause of the student's injury and will make your attorney's arguments in your defense much more persuasive. The legal guidelines to keep in mind before beginning any industrial education class or activity follow:

1. *Have a plan to prevent accidents.* Foresee and anticipate any potential risks or problem areas and have a plan to manage them.

2. *Follow and enforce your plan.* Most accidents occur not for lack of a plan but as a result of someone not following the plan.

3. *Provide for the health and safety of your students.* This is

especially important for industrial educators who have students working with potentially dangerous tools, equipment, and environments.

4. *Give proper instructions to your students.* The more dangerous the activity, the more time and effort the industrial education teacher should spend to make certain students fully understand the necessary directions and explanation.

Have a Plan to Prevent Accidents

An industrial education teacher took his class out on the lawn, away from the power machinery, to review a safety test the students had just completed. One boy in the class took with him a piece of sheet metal shaped like a knife that he had found in a bin in the shop. While the students were seated in a semicircle around the teacher, the student started flipping the knife into the ground. This action continued for quite a while, until eventually the knife struck a drawing board, was deflected, and caused an eye injury to another student. The court found sufficient evidence here from which a jury might infer that the teacher knew or should have known of the knife throwing, and that the teacher was inattentive and careless in failing to observe and stop the activity before the injury occurred.[2]

Invariably, one of the first questions a court will consider is whether or not a teacher had an adequate plan for supervision. Your plan should be well thought out and based on your past experiences and professional knowledge of the age group you teach and on any specific information you may have about individual students in your class.

Simply being absent from the classroom at the time of an accident does not necessarily make you its proximate cause. For example, consider again the anecdote that opened this chapter. The teacher is following a plan of supervison designed by the administration that places her in a position to observe most students passing in the halls between classes and at the same time have her back turned on a few students who had entered her classroom. If one student in the classroom injures another, the jury will probably consider you a teacher dutifully following school rules on supervision. The school attorney will argue that the school administration had foreseen the possibility of disruptions in the congested halls and therefore had a plan to place teachers in supervisory positions just outside their classrooms while leaving classrooms unsupervised for a short period of time. Most courts would agree that teachers cannot be everywhere at once and should be supervising the area where most students are congregated.

However, although the plan outlined by the administration may be good, information you have about the behavior of particularly disruptive students likely to cause injuries to others may lead you to question the school's plan and consider whether a reasonably prudent teacher should in this situation have another plan. If, for example, a student was a known bully and had injured other students in the past, your expected standard of care might be not to leave the student unsupervised, even briefly. Or, if sheet metal had been involved in previous student injuries, you might be liable for not having planned for safe and secure storage of sheet metal in your classroom.

A plan promulgated by your school administration or department may or may not relieve you of negligence. You must have your own plan designed and implemented to meet the foreseeable dangers unique in your classroom situation. Again, from a legal viewpoint, the law will hold you to a plan that provides for the standard of care commensurate with what a reasonable prudent industrial education teacher would have foreseen under the same or similar circumstances.

This question arose in a recent case settled out of court with a school district's insurance carrier. At the conclusion of an industrial arts class, a student handed a paintbrush to the teacher, whose standard technique of checking for proper cleaning involved brushing it on the student's cheek. As the startled student turned her head to avoid the brush, some of the bristles brushed her left eye. The injury resulted in severe abrasions to the eye. In relating this case, a representative of the insurance company commented that it would seem unlikely that a reasonably prudent teacher would have used that technique to demonstrate whether a paintbrush was clean and dry. Although the teacher had a plan to test the dryness of students' brushes, it was a poor plan and not well thought out. When developing a plan, you must consider not only your professional knowledge of your technical field but also your professional knowledge of human behavior as it relates to the age of your students.

Follow and Enforce Your Plan

A severe injury caused by a table-saw accident resulted in a judgment for a 14-year-old boy who had never before operated a power saw and received no instruction on one's operation. The teacher, who was outside the shop area at the time of the injury, knew that the classroom had a power saw and that the safety guard was not installed on the saw. The court held that the teacher breached the duty he owed the injured student to provide supervision at all times during the class period because of the presence of inherently dangerous equipment. Not only was the teacher outside the classroom at the time of the accident, but evidence showed that he frequently left the class at other times.[3]

Most teachers are found negligent not because they did not have a plan or did not foresee potential dangers, but because they did not *follow* the plan designed to prevent the possibility of injuries. An example appears in a case from Hawaii where three teachers did not show up for assigned supervision duties at a light show given to the student body in a dark auditorium. Some students began throwing things from the balcony, which resulted in an eye injury to a student sitting below. Testimony revealed that two of the teachers had forgotten about their supervisory assignment and, while they attended part of the assembly, had at the time of the injury been in the faculty room drinking coffee. The administration foresaw that a dark auditorium filled with students posed a potentially dangerous situation and assigned adequate supervision, but its well-devised plan went askew when the assigned teachers failed to attend the entire event. The jury, therefore, found the proximate cause of the injuries to be the lack of teacher supervision.[4]

An all-too-common example of this legal concept in industrial education classes appears in the discrepancy between the *plan* for using safety glasses and the *actual use* of safety glasses by both the teacher and students. All teachers must not only follow their own plans and have constant awareness of any dangers that may exist around them and their students, but they must also know about and take responsibility for following the plans for supervision assigned by their administration. Failing to follow a plan designed to prevent injuries will almost certainly result in a jury returning a negligence verdict.

Provide for Students' Health and Safety

A machine shop teacher was found negligent when a student in his class seriously injured himself while firing a model cannon at home. The student had constructed a bronze scale model of a Revolutionary War cannon as a class project in machine shop. When finished, the student took the cannon home and used a dismantled shotgun shell and additional powde, to muzzle load it. The cannon fired, blowing off two of the student's fingers and a portion of his wrist. Even though the injury-producing accident occurred after school hours and off school property, the teacher was found negligent for failing to warn the student of the danger of loading and firing a cannon.[5] Whenever students take part in school-related activities, whether on or off school property, the school holds responsibility for their health and safety.

Society, through its court system, places a high priority on the health and safety of its citizenry. There is little hope for a teacher responsible for an injury to a student who has not foreseen and accounted for a health or safety hazard related to any educational activity. The issue of foreseeability is central to determining negligence and especially important to industrial education teachers who work with equipment and processes that involve potential safety hazards.

The provision and use of safety glasses in industrial education classes gives an example of the legal concept of foreseeability. The most common injuries that occur in industrial education classes are eye injuries that could have been prevented with proper eye protection. Our research in pertinent legal cases, insurance claims, and records maintained by the National Society for the Prevention of Blindness revealed numerous eye injuries that could have been prevented by providing for the health and safety of students through the proper use of safety glasses.

The safety and proper guarding of equipment plays another important part in the legal concept of foreseeability. Industrial education, science, physical education, and athletics are school activities most likely to have equipment that unless maintained, operated, and used properly could lead to serious injuries. Equipment must be kept in safe operating condition, with appropriate safety or guarding devices intact.

In a case resulting from an accident in an industrial education class, another question that will invariably be asked is whether equipment or tools had proper guards and information available on manufacturers' safety updates. This is especially important in accidents that involve any machinery with moving parts, such as a table saw, jointer, or grinder. If a teacher allows use of machinery without the correct guard or safety equipment, the teacher has a greater likelihood of being found liable should an accident occur. Industrial education teachers should conduct regular inspections to insure that all tools and equipment are in safe operating condition.

Yet another area where foreseeability of injury plays an important role involves equipment that is inherently dangerous unless there is proper supervision during its use. The use of such equipment can give rise to what is referred to as the *attractive nuisance doctrine*. The attractive nuisance doctrine applies to those persons who maintain instruments or appliances on their premises of a character likely to attract children to play, or who permit dangerous conditions to remain with the knowledge that children have the habit of resorting to their premises for amusement. Industrial education classrooms abound with interesting-looking apparatuses and mechanical equipment that will attract a curious and adventuresome student who may have little or no knowledge of potential danger or hazards. An old table saw in the corner or a faulty electric motor in the storeroom provide examples of attractive nuisances. You should take reasonable precautions to assure that students could not operate them and become injured. An industrial education teacher can expect to be held strictly liable for all injuries that result from cases involving attractive nuisances.

Give Proper Instructions

A 14-year-old student brought action to recover for injuries when he severed several fingers from his left hand while operating a power saw in an industrial arts class. The court held that the teacher did not violate the standard of care required of him by law in instructing the student about the dangers of using a power saw and appropriate procedures to follow and that the student's injuries resulted from his own contributory negligence. The evidence showed that the industrial arts instructor gave a 20-minute review session on the proper use and operation of a power saw, including specific instruction regarding all necessary precautions. The teacher also required the student to review the safety instruction despite the student's protests that he already knew how to use the saw properly. The teacher then spent an additional 20 minutes using the student's wood to demonstrate proper measuring, cutting, and gluing of wood. He also told the class that he would make necessary cuts for any students who chose not to use the machinery.[6]

This case provides a good example of a teacher who not only took time to give proper instructions but also insisted on them over a student's protests. The demonstration added credibility to the teacher's being reasonably prudent and was strengthened by his offer to make cuts if students were unsure about their ability or understanding of the instructions. If the teacher had stopped after the 20-minute review session, he may or may not have met the standard of care required for proper instructions. By adding his demonstration and offer to make the cuts, however, he set up the school's defense of contributory negligence on the part of the student. The case, cited earlier, of the student injured while firing a model cannon gives an example of one that went against a teacher because the jury found that the teacher did not take the time and effort to provide proper instructions for safe use of the model cannon.

Every activity or class should begin with proper instructions. As a reasonably prudent professional, you must foresee the possibility of injuries that may result from the improper use of equipment, facilities, and activities. Teachers using inherently dangerous equipment or facilities have a responsibility to inform students of dangers and of precautions they should take to avoid injury. Written instructions are very helpful for classes and activities that involve operation of dangerous equipment and the possibility of severe injury. The existence of handouts to students and posted instructions in addition to verbal warnings and instructions will demonstrate to a jury that you made every effort to emphasize the importance of your instructions. Verbal instructions are always vulnerable to misunderstanding and misinterpretation or to students claiming that they did not hear what you said. Written instructions, documented in your lesson plans or course outline, will substantiate the fact that you gave proper instructions to all the students and will show exactly the material covered.

Keep track of absent students. Any absent on a day when you gave instructions should receive the instructions when they return to class. A good practice used by many industrial education teachers is to have every student pass a written test and demonstrate the ability to safely operate a machine before using that machine in class. As a general rule, the more dangerous the equipment or activity, the more effort and time you must devote to proper instructions.

While the many demands placed on industrial education teachers leave little time to think through all the legal ramifications of each situation, every teacher can be legally prepared by remembering the four legal guidelines discussed here: having a plan to prevent accidents, following the plan, providing for students' health and safety, and giving proper instruction. If you account for them, you can focus your efforts on the educational task at hand without having to shy away from new and exciting teaching techniques for fear of potential legal problems.

Liability of Others in Your Classroom

On many occasions, you may have paraprofessionals and nonprofessionals assist you in your industrial education class. These people usually do not have the professional training and background commensurate with a certified industrial education teacher and as a result are held to a lower standard of care. They are liable only for what a reasonably prudent person in their particular role—student teacher, aide, or volunteer—would have foreseen and provided for under the same or similar circumstances. As a consequence, the standard of care expected of the regular classroom teacher requires informing the nonprofessional of all known dangers and giving proper instruction on appropriate procedures. Write down your instructions and applicable procedures and then make sure you take time to completely orient nonprofessionals to the shop area. Emphasize the hidden dangers and hazardous areas likely to cause accidents and injuries. Review the proper use of all safety devices and guards on tools and machinery. Stress the safety rules most often broken by students and discuss effective ways you have found to remind students of these rules.

If, in your professional judgment, a student teacher is not prepared to handle the class alone, do not leave the room. If a qualified industrial education teacher is not available as a substitute teacher, it is good administrative policy to close the shop area and have students report to another room in the school. Even with a qualified substitute, the regular teacher's lesson plans must be complete and include instructions and classroom procedures related to safety. Work closely with paraprofessionals and nonprofessionals who come into your industrial education class. Know their abilities and limit their assignments to their areas of strength. If you use good professional judgment and show consistency in providing adequate instructions and warnings, you need not fear using others who can help or bring special expertise to your industrial education program.

Classroom Injuries

When a student is injured in your classroom, your method of attending to that student and the first steps you take must be those that a reasonably prudent industrial education teacher would take under the same or similar circumstances. If, for example, you have a first-aid card and you treat the injury as instructed in your first-aid class, you would be considered reasonable and prudent. If, however, you go beyond your knowledge of first aid or perform first aid improperly, you would fall below the standard of care expected of a first-aid giver treating an injury. Industrial educators without first-aid instruction also have a duty to act, but should use care not to do anything to the injured student that would exacerbate the injury or the student's condition. In other words, call for help.

In most school buildings, you will find school personnel with some medical knowledge who can provide emergency assistance. Although your standard of care may not require you to treat the injury, it surely demands that you properly attend to the situation. Most administrators have developed a policy on classroom injuries, and by following these procedures you will meet the standard of care expected of a regular classroom teacher.

Industrial education teachers commonly have bandages for students with small cuts or abrasions. However, having students treat themselves, does not always relieve the teacher of liability. You must follow your school policy on this matter. Some schools want all injuries treated by the school nurse or other qualified person, while others leave this decision to the teacher. Consider the age and maturity of your students in deciding whether to allow them to treat their own injuries. The younger the student, the more you should involve yourself and participate in treatment. Older students usually have some sense of how to provide themselves with adequate care and are expected to make reasonable decisions about their injuries. If you have any question about a student's injury and its treatment, call a parent or guardian. This is a good practice for medical reasons and it could also relieve you of liability in the case of a lawsuit. Have a plan of action for injuries so that when one does occur, you can react calmly and quickly, with the standard of care expected of a reasonably prudent industrial education teacher.

Following an accident, you should complete an accident report. Several good reasons exist for maintaining accurate records of any accidents in your classes. Accident reports can draw your attention to a hazardous condition in your lab, note external causes of an accident, and document all pertinent facts close to the time of the accident. Check with your school to see if it has a standard accident report form. Make several copies and keep them in a handy place.

Field Trips

Field trips offer great educational value and, when well planned and coordinated, they can be relatively safe and risk free. Industrial educators are usually very familiar with the potential dangers in their shop area, but they face an entirely different circumstance when they leave this known setting for the unknowns of a field-trip site. Factories and construction areas present many hidden and unknown dangers that must be found and addressed before you expose your class to the risks of an activity. Organizations that advertise for guests and sightseers are responsible for finding and giving notices of their unknown dangers, but organizations that seldom have visitors are held to a lower standard of care. Most of your field trips will likely be made to one of the latter sites and, therefore, will require more effort on your part to meet the standard of care expected of a reasonably prudent industrial educator taking a class on a field trip. You can meet this standard of care by making every effort to carry out the following three activities when planning a field trip.

First, educate yourself about the known and unknown dangers associated with your field-trip site. Take the time to make a personal on-site visit before you show up with your whole class. At a construction site, for example, make notes to yourself of areas to avoid and of any unforseen pitfalls likely to cause injury. Always get permission for the visit from the person in charge and ask specifically about potential hazards and danger to your students. Inform the person in charge of your class size and the age and maturity level of your students. Give opportunity to refuse your request for a field trip based on past experiences. Good communication with personnel at the site can signficantly reduce the probability of student accidents and injuries.

Second, your students should have a written statement describing what is required of them during the field trip and specific notice of the risks and dangers related to the visit. Go over this written statement orally, and leave time for questions and answers to make sure the students fully understand your directions and the risks they may encounter. If you have disciplinary measures for any violations of your rules, include them in your written and verbal instructions. These instructions will help protect students from a possible injury, and may also help you establish a strong case for contributory negligence and assumption of risk if a lawsuit arises.

Third, parents should be involved. Review with your school's legal counsel the validity of some type of hold-harmless agreement incorporated in a signed parental permission slip. In some cases, this may contractually relieve the district of liability for potential injuries. For long or overnight field trips, have a pretrip meeting with the students' parents and any volunteer escorts. Explain what the school expects of the students in areas such as independent sightseeing, prohibition of alcohol and drugs, review of itinerary, and the disciplinary procedures you intend to follow. Learn from the parents any hidden disabilities or idiosyncrasies of their children that you may have to deal with or that might without attention spoil the trip for others. As with students, communication with parents plays a vital role in the success of a good field trip.

Educational Malpractice

One of the first and leading cases in educational malpractice is *Peter W.* v. *San Francisco Unified School District*.[7] Peter W. received a high school diploma from the San Francisco schools. Although a California statute requires that graduates be able to read at over the eighth-grade level, Peter W. was illiterate. He sued the school district for negligence in not teaching him proper reading skills and for allowing him to graduate without them. The court's dismissal of the action was upheld on appeal and the school district was not held liable. This and subsequent malpractice cases against schools have all come to the same conclusion. The court's denials of claims have been based primarily on the following arguments:

1. There is lack of an appropriate standard of care against which to measure conduct.

2. A fear exists that recognition of the cause of action will cause a flood of litigation that would overburden the courts.

3. The award of monetary damages would be uncertain and inappropriate.

4. Litigation of such claims would lead to judicial interference in educational policy-making.

Although the weight of case authority indicates that industrial education teachers are unlikely to become involved in malpractice suits, one significant case involving industrial education was decided in favor of the student. A 1978 Oregon case involved a community college student with some basic welding training who wanted to qualify as an advanced welder. He contacted representatives of a college and was told that if he enrolled he would learn advanced welding, including metal inert gas welding (MIG) and tungsten inert gas welding (TIG), and the operation of a milling machine. Representatives of the college told the student that a milling machine was on order and would be available for use in instruction. The student, who attended the college for three consecutive terms, testified that he never received MIG or TIG training or instruction on a milling machine, which was still on order. The Oregon Supreme Court held for the student and found that there was evidence in the case on which a jury could conclude that the college's personnel made at least some representations in reckless disregard of whether it could perform. The court found this sufficient to prove "promissory fraud."[8]

In summary, it appears that an industrial educator is not likely to be held liable for teaching students poorly but should use care to teach competencies and curriculum as advertised. Review your course descriptions and brochures carefully and make sure you do what you say you will do and that you provide the equipment and tools you say you will.

Relieving Yourself of Liability

Occasionally, you will discover a hazardous situation in your teaching area. For example, one of the machines in your shop no longer seems safe to operate and, despite repeated attempts, you cannot get anyone to do anything about it. If a student receives an injury as a result of a known unsafe situation, who holds responsibility? Would it be the teacher or an administrator who was warned about the situation? In addition to protecting your students, an important question here involves what industrial education teachers must do to relieve themselves of liability and pass on the responsibility of the foreseeable danger to an administrator.

First, adequately document the problem that could lead to an injury. Your professional responsibility is to make certain your administrator fully understands the problem and knows the severity and complexities involved in the situation. A memorandum to your administrator that outlines the unsafe conditions and the materials or equipment needed to make it safe provides a good beginning. A photograph of the unsafe equipment may help clarify the problem. Good administrators encourage well-documented statements of existing problems because they can pass these along to higher administrators. Be thorough and complete. Don't be reluctant to inform your administrators of unsafe equipment that may lead to injuries.

Second, conduct an on-site inspection with your administrator. Demonstrate and show exactly how and where an injury may happen and what is needed to correct the problem. Prepare for the visit by obtaining advertisements of needed replacement equipment or modifications. Offer documentation of students injured on the equipment and anecdotes of students almost injured as a result of the unsafe condition. Know exactly what you want to tell your administrator and present it in a form understandable to a nonindustrial educator.

Third, follow up your efforts until the problem is finalized to the satisfaction of your professional judgment. Understand that as a professional industrial educator, you are considered expert in your subject area and directly responsible to your students for their health and safety. If your administrator is "working on the problem," stay with it and continue to check progress. If you have an inherently dangerous situation and a severe injury may result, do not permit anyone to use the equipment. In most cases, if an industrial education teacher adequately informs his or her administration of the unsafe condition and vigorously pursues resolution of the problem, the court will probably focus its attention on the administrator who held responsibility for allowing the situation to continue while knowing full well of the likelihood of a student injury.

Case Citations

[1] Horace Mann Insurance Co. v. Independent School District No. 656, 355 N.W. 2nd 413 (1983).

[2] Lilienthal v. San Leandro Unified School District, 293 P. 2nd 889 (1956).

[3] Lawrence v. Grant Parish School Board, 409 S. 2nd 1316 (1982).

[4] Viveiros v. State, 513 P. 2nd 487 (1973).

[5] Calandri v. Ione Unified School District, 33 Cal. Rptr. 333 (1963).

[6] Izard v. Hickory City Schools Board of Education, 315 S.E. 2nd 756 (1984).

[7] Peter W. v. San Francisco Unified School District, 131 Cal. Rptr. 854 (1976).

[8] Dizick v. Umqua Community College, 599 P. 2nd 444 (1979).

Resources

American Vocational Association. *Let's Teach Safety.* Arlington, Va.: American Vocational Association, 1980.

Firenze, Robert J., and James B. Walters. *Safety and Health for Industrial/Vocational Education: For Supervisors and Instructors.* Washington, D.C.: U.S. Department of Health and Human Services, 1981.

Kigin, Denis J. *Teacher Liability in School-Shop Accidents.* Ann Arbor, Mich.: Prakken Publications, Inc., 1973.

National School Safety Center. *School Safety Legal Anthology.*

Sacramento, Calif.: Pepperdine University Press, 1985.

National School Safety Center. *School Safety and the Legal Community*. Sacramento, Calif.: Pepperdine University Press, 1985.

Strong, Merle E. *Accident Prevention Manual for Training Programs*. Chicago, Ill.: American Technical Society, 1975.

CHAPTER 2
Product and Service Liability

As part of a community college automotive class, students perform repair jobs for the local community. The students enjoy the chance to do some "real" work and the customers appreciate having repairs done without a labor charge. Everything seemed to work pretty well until last week, when a neighbor of one of the college's teachers brought in a car to have the brake pads replaced. After the work was done, he complained that the brakes squealed every time he stepped on them. Together with his students, the instructor carefully checked all the work and found nothing wrong. The customer picked up the car and everything seemed fine. A couple of days later, though, the squeal returned louder than ever, and the brake pedal went all the way to the floor whenever he stopped the car. Now, the customer is angry and wants the school to pay for a complete brake job, including a new master cylinder. The instructor knows his students did good work and didn't cause the master cylinder problem, but the customer plans to visit the department chairman and threatens to take the instructor to court.

The instructor has heard that the construction teacher had a similar problem when his class built a garage for someone in the community. Who should pay for the repairs? Will the school's insurance cover it? What would have happened if the customer was injured? Will incidents like this jeopardize a policy of having students make repairs for the community? Should students do repairs only on students' or teachers' cars? Should the customer sign a waiver or release form?

These are just a few of the questions that can arise when an educational program provides a service or produces a product for the general public. This chapter will give an overview of school insurance coverage, the legal basis for tort liability, and implications and recommendations for industrial education teachers.

Legal and Insurance Protection

Whenever an industrial education teacher and students interact with the general public, they must observe appropriate legal, regulatory, and insurance guidelines. Regardless of whether the general public pays for a product or service, the industrial education teacher has a legal responsibility for students' actions. An understanding and working knowledge of legal, insurance, and other relevant regulations can help educators design programs that offer the maximum educational benefit and protection for both the industrial education program and the general public.

Legal Protection

Industrial educators who plan and implement educational programs that involve the general public must consider potential liability. Liability issues hold even greater importance for activities that include the public than for more typical activities that involve only the teacher and students. When planning activities that involve the general public, you must address the same legal considerations you would account for in other class activities.

Any claim of negligence or liability will be judged on what a reasonable and prudent industrial education teacher would do in the same or a similar situation. In planning activities that involve the public, you must make sure that you stay within the scope of your duty. An industrial education teacher who has a class build small garden sheds as part of a planned educational program would be operating within his or her scope of duty. On the other hand, an industrial education teacher who with students repairs neighbors' or friends' cars on the weekend may not be operating within the scope of duty. He or she, therefore, may not have claim to insurance or legal defense by the school district.

To plan activities that involve the general public and protect your programs from claims of negligence and liability, you must minimize your risks while maximizing educational benefits to your students. Minimize potential risk by applying the same guidelines

introduced in our chapter on safety and liability:
- Have a plan for supervision.
- Follow your plan.
- Consider health and safety issues.
- Give proper instructions.

Planning for Supervision

One of the first questions you'll hear if a problem arises with a class activity that involves the general public is whether you had a plan for supervision. Such activity may be far more complex and will require more planning and closer supervision than an activity in which a product never leaves your class. Not only does your legal standard of care increase, but your program's reputation with the public has greater vulnerability. In addition to supervising student activities, you may also need a well-thought-out plan for proper supervision for the purchase and use of materials or supplies required for the activity. Careful checking of all student purchases can prevent the use of inferior or unsuitable parts or equipment. You may need to have a customer leave a car or appliance in your class for a period of time. You must make allowances for the security and safety of any items left in your custody.

Your plan for supervision may not require your constant presence and supervision of all students while they work. You should determine, however, where your supervision is most needed, based on your past experience and professional knowledge of your students' abilities and the nature of the class activities. It is especially important that you have a plan to supervise activities with the greatest potential risk. You must supervise and check a completed project before it goes back to the owner or into operation.

For example, if your class repairs audiovisual equipment for the school, you might check each item for safe operation before your students release it. If your class builds tool sheds for the community, you may want to check with customers and inspect jobs on a regular basis. Proper supervision is essential to safety and liability considerations of any program that provides a service or produces a product for the general public.

Following Your Plan

Simply having a plan for supervision of class activities that involve the general public is not enough to protect you, your students, and your program. You must follow through and carry out your plan. Incorporate a checklist or form that provides a written record of your supervision at different points in the activity. By documenting important steps, you are less likely to forget or overlook something in the midst of the many other activities going on in your class. A completed checklist will impress the customer, who will leave confident that the job was properly supervised. In the unlikely event of a lawsuit or insurance claim, the checklist can show that you met a standard of care for supervision commensurate with that of a reasonably prudent industrial education teacher. Always keep a copy for your records—it will serve you well in your class planning, with the public, and, if needed, in a court of law. Having a plan for supervision that is not followed is tantamount to having no supervision. Be sure to take the time necessary to follow a consistent plan that attends to risks foreseeable in an activity.

Considering Health and Safety

Proper safety instruction forms an important part of all industrial education activities. In planning activities that involve the public, you should carefully consider the foreseeability of any health or safety problem related to students' activity. As business invitees, customers must receive warning of all unknown dangers on the premises. Tools and equipment laying around, unguarded dangerous machines, oil on the floor, or exhaust fumes represent just a few examples of situations against which the public—as well as your students—must have protection. You must also observe all pertinent local, state, and federal safety regulations and codes that apply to your activity. For example, if your class constructs a house or any other structure, students should observe all pertinent safety regulations. The job site should be kept safe and free of debris and hazardous materials. Students should use safety glasses and other required safety equipment. If you do not have the required expertise, experience, or license, any specialized work, such as electrical wiring, should be done by someone else licensed and qualified in accordance with local and state regulations. Students can still benefit from observing the work and learning correct procedures.

You should carefully screen for potential safety hazards any class activities that involve the general public. As an example, if your students tune up lawnmowers for the community, perform a careful safety check before returning serviced lawnmowers to customers. If a class activity presents a clear safety hazard, with a clear possibility of injury, select a different, safer activity that provides the same or similar educational benefits. If you must choose between a student's education and a student's safety, always go with safety. No educational benefit warrants serious risk to the health and safety of your students or the public you serve.

Giving Proper Instructions

In a class activity that involves the general public, not only must you give students proper instructions, but you also must communicate certain information to the public. Do not depend on verbal instructions alone—they are always more vulnerable to misinterpretation and forgetfulness. Document your instructions to your students and your communications with the public, through carefully prepared written materials. These should include such items as customer waiver or release forms, work orders, job estimates, working drawings, or customer billings that detail work completed and materials used. While a school program cannot legally ask a customer to waive or release the right to sue a school for negligence, you can use a waiver to inform the customer of the purpose of the activity and to limit your liability in the event of an injury or damages to property. A release can also detail an activity's procedures and costs.

If you prepare a waiver form, be sure to include a statement that explains the purpose of the activity. Emphasize that your program is primarily an educational activity designed to give students learning experiences. Use forms as similar as possible to those actually used in the trades. In addition to giving a professional appearance and valuable information to the customer, use of waiver forms provides educational benefits to your students. Have your waiver forms reviewed by your school attorney and administration.

Instruct students to prepare a work order or job estimate sheet. This will give to them experience in documenting and communicating on the job and keep your customer well informed. When a job is completed, have your students prepare a final billing. Even if there is no charge for labor, students should detail every part or material cost for the customer. Keep copies of all correspondence with customers. When possible, have the customer meet and talk to the student or students who were responsible for the service or product. This practice personalizes the activity and greatly enhances the learning and public value of your program. Communication is vital to a vigorous and enterprising public service program. Spend time on the paperwork necessary to do the job. Lackadaisical or careless attention to this part of your program can result in poor public relations, student injuries, and lawsuits.

Legal Statutes and Regulations

Any industrial education class involved with the general public must observe the legal statutes and regulations that apply to a private business. This not only protects the industrial education program, but it can also help students learn pertinent regulations and the reasons for observing them. State contractor licensing laws provide one example of legal statutes and regulations that apply to industrial education carpentry and construction classes. According to the 1985 National Association of Home Builders' *Report of All State Builder Licensing Laws*, all but 17 states have statewide builder licensing requirements.[1] The report does not indicate any exemptions for educational programs involved in construction or home remodeling. It offers an excellent resource for industrial education teachers who need to find licensing requirements for their state. As an example, state law in Oregon requires that schools that engage in home construction or remodeling register with the Builder's Board. Oregon Revised Statute 701 specifically identifies a school district as a builder in Provision 701.005(b), where it states that a builder may be "a school district, as defined in ORS 332.002, that permits students to construct a structure as an educational experience to learn building techniques and, upon completion of the structure, the district sells the completed structure."[2] An Oregon school that registers as a builder must pay an annual $55 fee, post a surety bond of $5,000 (an existing bank account can be used), and show evidence of public liability and property damage insurance.

Registration requirements and fees vary widely from state to state. In Michigan, any builder engaged in residential construction or remodeling must register with the Residential Builders' and Maintenance and Alteration Contractors' Board by paying an annual registration fee of $40. Other states, such as North Carolina, have a staggered fee schedule determined by the value of the construction project. Most school building projects qualify for the minimum registration fee. Some states require that any construction valued above a specified amount be performed by certified builders who have passed a state examination. Industrial education carpentry or construction teachers should check with their state builder-licensing agency regarding requirements and fees. Most schools will already have the necessary insurance coverage and sufficient funds for a surety bond. Payment of the yearly fee legally meets this state requirement, helps protect the program, and serves as a good model for students.

A number of local building codes and regulations also apply to any construction or remodeling done by an industrial education class. Before beginning any class project that involves the general public, the teacher and class should research and identify pertinent codes or regulations. Spend class time learning the codes and regulations and their importance to the protection of society. Local communities typically have code and permit requirements for construction, electrical, and plumbing work. Industrial education teachers should contact a local building official or inspector for detailed information. The inspector will probably be willing to speak to your students and help them meet code and permit requirements. Industrial education classes help future builders and homeowners become familiar with code requirements and the rationale behind them. They also provide standards to determine whether a job is performed negligently.

Insurance Protection

All secondary and postsecondary schools maintain insurance coverage to protect against potential losses. One type of coverage that schools carry is general liability insurance, which protects the school from the claims of a third party. Schools may purchase it from an insurance company or can set aside money for self-insurance. Any claim that results from a class project would most likely be covered by the school's general liability coverage. If a school receives a claim for damages that result from an activity that involves the general public, it would be protected against any claims covered in its insurance policy. Refer to Chapter 4 for information on insurance and for specific recommendations on working successfully with your insurance company.

Implications for Industrial Educators

Despite potential risks, an increasing number of industrial education programs engage in class projects that involve the general public. These projects include constructing a house, mass-producing an item for sale, or providing a service such as auto or microcomputer repair. Although these activities pose potential risks, there are good reasons for incorporating them into the industrial education curriculum. Carefully planned class activities that involve industrial education students with the public can

- provide educational benefits to the students.
- improve community and school relations.
- provide service to the community, public, or school.
- generate additional sources of funding.

Educational Benefits

Good class projects and activities that involve the general public can give students educational experiences that relate very closely to actual work experience. Research shows that learning through theory and practice greatly enhances the students' interest and motivation as well as their ability to grasp concepts and apply them to the workplace.

For example, most of the 4,000 students at Clover Park Vocational-Technical Institute in Tacoma, Washington, take part in educational programs that operate as businesses producing products or services. In a facility that resembles a modern shopping center, the students run automotive service and electronic repair centers, a plant shop, and a deli. There's even a 64-foot tugboat operated by the marine mechanics students in the Puget Sound.[3] Through such programs students can gain valuable skills in customer relations, project planning, management, organization, and problem solving—all skills effectively learned in a class project that involves the general public.

It is important in designing class activities to consider both the educational needs of the students and the needs of the public. An educational program designed solely to meet the commercial needs of the public may not operate within the scope of duty of a public institution and may conflict with the interests of businesses operating in the public sector. As an example, a high school automotive program that does extensive repairs on a walk-in basis may present unfair competition to local repair shops. The primary purpose of the high school auto repair program should be to provide students with educational experiences, not to repair cars for the general public. Industrial education teachers should try to arrange jobs that give students varied and appropriate learning experiences.

Public Relations

Class projects that involve industrial education students with the general public provide an excellent opportunity for good community/school relations. The building trades program at Sevier County Vocational Center in Tennessee built a temporary shelter for runaway youth and juvenile offenders. They worked with local government officials, architects, and the business community to design and construct a 2,000-square-foot house. As a result of the project, enrollment in the building trades program increased, local contractors gained confidence in the program, and the class provided a valuable community service.[4] This shows just one example of the positive public relations that can be generated by successful class projects for the general public. On the other hand, a poor building trades program reduces the public's confidence in the local schools and can contribute to the defeat of school budgets and bond elections.

Service to the Public

As in the preceding example, class projects for the general public or for the school can provide a valuable service. The Tippecanoe Building Trades Program in Lafayette, Indiana, worked with the local board of realtors to renovate older homes in distressed areas of the city. While the program's primary objective was to give students sufficient home-building experience, its by-product was a valuable community service that received a special award from the Lafayette Chamber of Commerce.[5] A good program also gives a community a better-prepared work force, which could contribute to attracting new business and industry.

Generating Supplemental Funding

Class projects for the general public can also provide additional or supplemental funding. Some industrial classes use funds generated in class projects to purchase equipment or supplies. Some automotive progams use funds raised in their auto repair projects to finance Vocational Industrial Clubs of America (VICA) activities. Not only do these activities motivate students, but the money they generate returns to the students in ways that provide additional educational experiences. Many industrial arts classes make use of a mass-production project whose products are sold to the general public to recover material costs and generate a profit that goes toward purchase of additional supplies. Learning to work with others as a team member is essential to keeping a job. There's no better way to learn valuable interpersonal skills than through a meaningful class activity under the skilled leadership of a good teacher.

Recommendations

Industrial education activities that involve the general public must be designed to minimize risks and maximize educational benefits to students. The following recommendations will help industrial education teachers and administrators design, implement, and administer such activities.

Maximizing Educational Benefit

The primary purpose of industrial education programs—whether industrial arts, industrial vocational, or technical education—is not to produce a product for or deliver a service to the general public. Rather, their goal is to provide educational benefits to students. Activities that involve the general public can provide educational benefits only when they make up part of a planned curriculum designed to help students accomplish specific objectives. One educational benefit to be gained through involvement with the general public is practice at interacting with the consumer. Communicating with members of the public to determine job requirements, ordering materials and supplies, handling billing and orders, and trouble-shooting are all important job-preparation skills. Take care to design industrial education activities that optimize the achievement of these important objectives.

For example, an automotive program may hold as one objective attaining the ability to work with a customer in a realistic job setting. Your students may be able to meet the objective of interacting with the public by doing routine oil changes, lubes, or tune-ups—rather than costly and risky engine overhauls or brake jobs. You may consider the educational objectives involved in overhauling engines or performing brake jobs best learned in a controlled environment on equipment that belongs to the school. By carefully selecting educational activities to match your program's educational objectives, you can minimize risks while maximizing the educational benefits for your students.

Documentation

Most existing industrial education programs that involve the general public show a major weakness in their lack of documentation. In preparing students for jobs, you must stress the importance of documentation. The preparation of work orders, job estimates, customer billings, and permit or license applications all constitute part of the work of business and industry. Not only will your students learn the importance of good record-keeping and writing skills, but you will establish good records to deal with an unsatisfied customer or insurance claim.

Communication

If you decide to include a class activity that involves the general public, communicate your plans with everyone involved. Let your administration, insurance company, school attorney, and advisory committee know what your students will do, why they are doing it, and when. By carefully documenting plans, you will establish that the class activity lies within the scope of your duty and plays a part in your planned educational program. You will also establish the tacit approval of your administration. Rather than fear that your description of the activity will jeopardize your program, view it as an opportunity to recieve additional assistance in planning and implementation. Your administration may be able to help you meet legal or insurance requirements. Your advisory committee may provide helpful resources. Good communication can hold the key to a successful activity that promotes your programs and your students.

Observing Pertinent Regulations

Whenever an industrial education class produces a product or delivers a service for the general public, it has the same level of responsibility a private enterprise would have. Whether students build a garden shed or a house, or repair a car, they must identify and observe pertinent regulations. In almost any area of production or service, you'll find local, state, or federal regulations or guidelines. As future workers or consumers, your students should learn the content and importance of pertinent regulations.

Resource People

In activities that involve the general public, you'll find many resource people who can enhance your instruction. Your local building official or inspector, a representative from Underwriters Laboratory, or a representative of the Better Business Bureau may be able to supply you with information and materials related to class activities. They may also offer to make a presentation to your class. A local electrical inspector can inform students of inspection procedures and the latest code changes, and can describe actual electrical inspections.

Professional trade organizations offer another valuable resource. As an example, the National Institute for Automotive Service Excellence (A.S.E.) offers voluntary certification for automobile technician training programs. Based on an on-site team evaluation, your automotive program can receive national certification in any or all of eight technical specialty areas. The A.S.E. inspection can help you evaluate the operation of your automotive repair or service activity, identify areas for facility or curriculum improvement, add to the prestige and credibility of your program, and give your graduates a competitive edge in the job market.

Use of resource people enriches your program; it also helps your resource people do their jobs. Strong industrial education programs are in their best interest. An investment in tomorrow's workers and consumers can pay off in greater consumer knowledge and a better quality product or service.

References

[1]National Association of Home Builders. *Review of All State Builder Licensing Laws.* Washington, D.C.: National Association of Home Builders, 1985.

[2]Oregon Homebuilders Act, OR. Code Ann. Section 701-005-992 (1983).

[3]Crewdson, A. "School in a Real-World Setting." *Vocational Education Journal* 59 (1984), no. 6, 33-35.

[4]Ball, N. L. "A Place Built by Youth." *Vocational Education Journal* 60 (1985), no. 5, 55.

[5]Bockert, D. L. "Building Better Neighborhoods." *Vocational Education Journal* 60 (1985), no. 4, 43-44.

Resources

Littrell, J. J. *From School to Work.* South Holland, Ill.: Goodheart-Willcox, 1984.

Umstaddt, W. D. "Product Servicing Curriculum: A Rationale and Structure." *Journal of Industrial Teacher Education* 16 (1979), no. 3, 12-20.

CHAPTER 3
Cooperative Work Experience

Susan has been actively involved in amateur radio since she was in seventh grade, so the high school electronics teacher is well aware of her talents and interest in communications and electronics. When Susan asks about the cooperative work experience program, the teacher knows just the placement for her. Mike, the owner of Mike's TV Shop, asked just last week about the possibility of having a student help him in his TV repair business. Susan is delighted with the opportunity to work in a "real" shop and Mike seems pleased with Susan. The TV shop is some distance from school, so Susan's teacher asks Bob, a new sophomore in the program, if Susan can ride with him on the way to his co-op placement at a fast-food restaurant.

On supervisory visits, the teacher finds everything going well with Mike, Susan, and Bob, until she drives past the shop late one evening and sees Susan and Mike still working. Feeling concerned, the teacher decides to talk with Mike about it. The next day on her visit to Mike's shop, she learns that Susan and Bob are in the hospital with injuries from an accident in Bob's car on the way to the shop. Later, she learns that Bob has a drinking problem and was drinking just before the accident, in which he ran a stop sign and broadsided a bakery truck two blocks from Mike's shop.

In addition to showing a classic example of "everything that can go wrong will go wrong," the incident described above forces us to examine our legal responsibilities in a cooperative education program. Cooperative education programs move industrial education out of the school and into the community and thus subject it to many different legal statutes and regulations. In cooperative work experience programs, a special three-way partnership is formed between the student, the school, and the employer. Each partner has a legal duty and responsibility to the others. Each partner also has differing and sometimes conflicting objectives. The school or college that uses cooperative work experience programs has a primary obligation of providing students with educational experience. The employer's primary objective involves operating a successful and profitable business. The student's primary objective is to gain educational experience not available in the traditional school setting. When these objectives conflict with each other and the laws that govern employment and education, several legal issues surface. In this chapter, we will explore the legal issues related to industrial education cooperative work experience in such areas as employment practices, labor regulations, insurance, taxes, and transportation.

The Law

Child Labor Regulations

A working knowledge of federal and state labor laws governing the employment and work experiences of students is important to any industrial education teacher who places students in cooperative work experience. You can easily find the information you need through federal and state child labor offices. Not only will materials from these sources help you comply with pertinent laws and regulations, but you can also use them as resource materials for your students. A United States Department of Labor publication, "Child Labor Requirements in Nonagricultural Occupations"[1] provides a good overview of federal guidelines given in the Fair Labor Standards Act. This act sets standards based on the minor's age and working conditions. It identifies occupational fields and specific jobs that minors may or may not be employed in, with exceptions for student learners in approved school-supervised and school-administered work experience and career exploration programs. Awareness of these career fields and their exceptions for student learners is important to any teacher placing and supervising students in cooperative work experience programs.

The Child Labor Act sets the following hour and time standards under which 14- and 15-year-old minors may *not* be employed:

● during school hours, except as provided for in work experience and career exploration programs,

- before 7 a.m. or after 7 p.m., except from June 1 through Labor Day when minors may work until 9 p.m.,
- more than 3 hours per day on school days,
- more than 18 hours during school weeks,
- more than 8 hours per day on nonschool days, and
- more than 40 hours per week in nonschool weeks.

The Child Labor Act also provides a minimum age of 18 years for any nonagricultural occupations that the Secretary of Labor declares particularly hazardous for 16- and 17-year-old persons or detrimental to their health and well-being. The minimum age applies even when the minor is employed by a parent or person standing in place of a parent. It is important, therefore, to be aware of 17 hazardous occupations defined by federal legislation. Briefly and broadly stated, they include work that involves explosives, motor vehicles, mining, logging and saw milling, radioactive substances, slaughtering, manufacturing kindred products, wrecking operations, roofing, excavation, and the operation of some power-driven machinery in a number of specifically named occupations, such as those using cranes or hoists.

Seven of the 17 hazardous occupations have exemptions if a student is enrolled in a course of study and training in a cooperative vocational training program under a recognized state or local education authority or in a substantially similar program conducted by a private school. In addition, the student must be employed under a written agreement that provides that

- the work of the student learner in occupations declared particularly hazardous must be incidental to the training;
- such work must take place intermittently, for short periods of time, and under the direct and close supervision of a qualified and experienced person;
- safety instructions must be given by the school and correlated by the employer with on-the-job training; and
- a schedule of organized and progressive work processes to be performed on the job must be prepared.

The student learner exemption may be revoked in any situation where reasonable safety precautions are not observed.

For each violation of federal child labor provisions, employers may be subject to a civil money penalty of up to $1,000. In case of willful violation of these provisions, the law also provides for a fine of up to $10,000 or imprisonment of not more than six months, or both.

State laws will differ slightly depending on the occupations particular to a given state. Remember that your program must comply with both federal and state laws. If a conflict exists between them, federal law usually supercedes state law. In some places, however, state law may be more limiting than federal law, in which case state law takes precedence. Where these matters are unclear, consult your federal and state child labor office.

Insurance and Taxes

Responsibility for providing worker's compensation insurance to cover an on-the-job accident belongs to the legal employer of the student worker. Legal employment is determined by whether the student received pay for work performed at the training station. Paid work experience requires the employer to provide worker's compensation insurance coverage. The school holds responsibility for insurance in nonpaid employment. For additional information on worker's compensation, refer to Chapter 4.

Employees usually insure paid work experience students in the same manner as regular employees. Also, the same coverage applies to employment during and after school hours.

State laws usually make special provisions for providing nonpaid students with insurance protection while on the job. Students must be enrolled in an approved work experience program for coverage under these provisions.

Students are considered legal employees of the local school district while on nonpaid work assignments. To cover them, the school district must apply for coverage with its state accident insurance fund or a designated private carrier. Schools must submit to the insurance carrier for approval a list of nonpaid student workers with their places of work and job assignments. Upon the insurance carrier's approval, the school pays premiums and insurance coverage takes effect. Insurance premiums are computed on an assumed-wage basis.

Your school's insurance carrier can provide a complete explanation of the procedures and conditions for insuring work experience students. The carrier will gladly have a representative meet with you to review insurance coverage as it relates to your cooperative work experience program. For more information related to insurance and industrial education programs, refer to Chapter 4.

The Federal Unemployment Tax Act of 1971 (FUTA) specifically excluded cooperative work experience students from receiving unemployment benefits, thereby relieving employers from paying unemployment taxes on their wages. While the Act of 1971 only excluded students younger than 22, it was recently amended to eliminate the age limitation and thereby to except all co-op programs regardless of the students' ages. However, not all states have amended their laws to be consistent with the federal law, so you should contact your state employment office for the most recent information. This is especially important to postsecondary programs.

On the other hand, all paid work experience students must have social security taxes withheld from their paychecks by their employer. If a student cannot use federal form W-4E, the employer must withhold both state and federal income taxes from the paycheck, as well.

Transportation and Tort Liability

Assigning students to use their own cars to transport others to work outside of school is always a concern to teachers. If an accident occurs, the question of negligence regarding the person who arranged the transportation invariably arises. The court tests this question, as it tests other questions of negligence, by asking what a reasonably prudent professional would have foreseen under the same or similar circumstances and whether the person involved met the standard of care expected, commensurate with the risks involved. In other words, what should the reasonably prudent work experience coordinator have done before the accident to prevent it from happening or, if it does happen, to relieve the school, coordinator, and teacher of liability for negligence?

Many schools already have a policy for students driving their own cars for school-sponsored activities or events. You may be able to use or adapt that policy for your cooperative work experience program. The policy might include having:

- proof that the student driving has a valid driver's license;
- proof of adequate insurance on the car used;
- a signed statement from a parent or guardian giving the student permission to drive other students;

● a statement signed by a parent or guardian permitting his or her child or ward to ride with another student; and

● a record of every driving student's accidents and moving violations. (Check with local law-enforcment agencies for this information, which is public record—no invasion of privacy is involved.)

In addition to these guidelines, you should keep accurate records and follow carefully the plan you adopt. If an accident occurs, write down everything you can remember about the events leading to and following it. Careful attention to a plan that includes these precautions will normally result in your school not being the proximate cause of an accident involving a student-driven vehicle.

Equal-Access Requirements

All placements for cooperative work experience are subject to the legal requirements of the equal-access and equal-opportunity laws, including Title VI of the Civil Rights Act of 1964 and Title IX of the Education Amendments of 1972. Cooperative education programs must ensure that every student has the same opportunity to participate in cooperative work experience regardless of race, color, national origin, sex, or handicap.

You can facilitate compliance with equal opportunity requirements by requesting written assurances of nondiscrimination from every employer you use for cooperative work placements. Local school districts can further meet this requirement by including a nondiscrimination statement on all standard training agreements, training plans, and contracts.

Specific guidelines for meeting equal access requirements in cooperative work experience programs include

● listing jobs and referring students for job interviews without regard to race, color, national origin, sex, or handicap;

● equal treatment of all cooperative work experience students with regard to task assignment, hours of employment, responsibility levels, and pay;

● prohibition against honoring any prospective employer's request for students of a particular sex, race, color, or nationality; and

● an affirmative action plan that informs and assists minority students in cooperative work experience programs.

Implications for the Industrial Educator

Cooperative work experience is increasingly used as a valuable addition to industrial education programs. Many skills are best learned on the job with all the problems and constraints inherent in a "for-profit" operation. Research demonstrates that cooperative work experience programs can give vocational education programs higher rates of return on an educational investment than other types of instruction. Indeed, one of the primary education thrusts of the 1980s has been the emergence of new partnerships and cooperative efforts between industry and education. These cooperative programs have a variety of forms and names. Cooperative work experience (CWE), distributive education (DE), part-time industrial cooperative education, and diversified occupations (DO) are some of the common titles used in schools. The Carl D. Perkins Vocational Education Act of 1984, P.L. 98-524, provides the following definition:

> The term *cooperative education* means a method of instruction of vocational education for individuals who, through written cooperative arrangements between the school and employers, receive instruction, including required academic courses and related vocational instruction by alternation of study in school with a job in any occupational field, but the two experiences must be planned and supervised by the school and employers so that each contributes to the student's education and to his or her employability. Work periods and school attendance may be on alternative half days, full days, weeks, or other periods of time in fulfilling the cooperative program.[2]

This definition provides a basis for developing cooperative work experience programs that will give your students quality educational experiences and help you manage your legal risks. Whether you have an on-going cooperative work experience program or consider implementing a new one, four issues can help bring success (1) coordination and communication, (2) a signed training agreement, (3) a training plan, and (4) effective evaluation.

Coordination and Communication

Good communication and coordination plays an essential role in the partnership formed in a cooperative work experience program. Whenever you arrange to have a student leave school for an educational work experience, these factors are key concerns. You may work in a school district or college that has a coordinator or administrator of cooperative work experience. In that case, you, as the industrial education teacher, will serve as a resource in identifying placement sites, developing a training plan, and, possibly, supervising the student.

In addition to state and federal legislation related to work experience, your school district or college will have policies on student placement, hours, transportation, and other related issues. If you hold responsibility for your cooperative work experience program, meet with your administration to review your school's policies.

Local advisory committees can serve as a communications and coordination link with employers. State and local advisory committees are required under the Carl D. Perkins Vocational Education Act of 1984, P.L. 98-524, for any programs that receive federal vocational monies. In addition to assisting with program planning, facility and equipment planning, public relations, and other functions, your advisory committee can provide valuable assistance to your cooperative work experience program. An advisory committee can help your program gain access to equipment and technology otherwise unavailable, identify potential training placements, assess local training needs, and help coordinate training plans between the school and training site. If you don't already have a local advisory committee, start one. Information on how to start and maintain a successful advisory committee is available from your state advisory committee or council for vocational education.

Keep the lines of communication open. The cooperative work experience coordinator or teacher, guidance personnel, administration, employers, advisory committee, and students all must be aware of your policies and procedures.

The Training Agreement

A training agreement can clarify the duties and responsibilities of each of the participants in cooperative education's three-way partnership between the student, school, and the employer. One key component in cooperative education as defined in federal legislation is the "written cooperative arrangement." Such a written arrangement or agreement is required for any federally funded program. Regardless of the funding source, you should prepare a written training agreement—typically one or two pages long—for every student in a cooperative work experience program. The training agreement should be composed cooperatively and signed by the employer, the coordinator or teacher, the student, and the student's parent or guardian. The agreement should clearly outline the employer's and student's responsibilities to the program and the legal conditions of the student's employment. Many schools refer to the training agreement as a "memorandum of understanding." After you develop a standard training agreement, have it reviewed by your school district's attorney, advisory committee, and school administrator. You should take care to accurately represent your program capabilities. Be sure that you really intend to include everything you promise or imply will be provided by the institution or employer.

The training agreement should include information about the student, school, and employer; length and times of training; wage and working-condition information; detailed responsibilities of the student, school, and employer; and signatures of the involved parties. If your school or college does not have a standard training agreement form, you can obtain samples from your state department of vocational education.

The Training Plan

Another key component of the Perkins Act definition of cooperative education requires that students receive planned and coordinated instruction both in school and at the training site. As with any other educational experience, every student's cooperative work experience must have specific goals and learning objectives. An added requirement for planning cooperative work experience involves coordination of each student's in-school instruction with his or her on-the-job experiences. A training plan helps organize the instruction and correlate classroom instruction with on-the-job experiences. A training plan has greater detail than a training agreement and focuses on the delivery of instruction to work experience students. Factors considered in each student's training plan should include career objectives, planned learning experiences in the classroom and on the job, safety considerations, and evaluation strategies.

Ideally, each student's placement should relate to his or her career interests and objectives. Within the limitations of available training sites and each student's interests and abilities, the coordinator or teacher has the difficult task of matching students with training sites. The coordinator or teacher also has a legal and ethical responsibility to ensure that the training site is a safe environment and that the student's abilities indicate likelihood of successful job performance.

Evaluation

A fourth key component of cooperative work experience programs involves evaluation. The Perkins Act definition of cooperative education specifically states that it must be planned and supervised by the school and employers. The student learner's progress in cooperative work experience should be systematically evaluated and monitored. Individual states, school districts, or colleges often specify the minimum number of visits each student must receive and the maximum number of students a coordinator or teacher may evaluate. For specific regulations and guidelines, check with your state department of education.

The industrial education teacher, cooperative work experience coordinator, and employer should all take an active role in evaluation. The evaluation process and procedures should be based on learning objectives specified in the training plan. Examples of specific criteria that might be included in the evaluation process are the quality and quantity of work, student dependability and initiative, and safety practices. The content and form of the evaluation instrument should be compatible with the grading process used in your school or college. Be sure to provide regular feedback and communication between the school, employer, and student.

A well-planned cooperative work experience can easily prove valuable and rewarding. This is especially true for industrial education students, who work with changing technology, equipment, and processes. Regardless of whether your school or college has an existing cooperative education program and coordinator, the legal issues covered here will help you develop and implement educationally and legally sound cooperative work experience programs for your industrial education students.

References

[1]U.S. Department of Labor. *Child Labor Requirements in Nonagricultural Occupations.* Child Labor Bulletin No. 101. Washington, D.C.: U.S. Department of Labor, 1978.

[2]Carl D. Perkins Vocational Education Act of 1984, Section 2, 20 U.S.C. Section 2301 et seq. (1984).

Resources

Evans, R.N., and E.L. Herr. *Foundations of Vocational Education.* Columbus, Ohio: Charles E. Merrill Co., 1978.

Goldstein, M.B. "Law and Ethics in Cooperative Education." *Journal of Cooperative Education* 20 (1984), no. 2, 39-48.

Littrell, J.J. *From School to Work.* South Holland, Ill.: Goodheart-Willcox Co., 1984.

Mason, R.E., and P.G. Haines, *Cooperative Occupational Education and Work Experience in the Curriculum.* Danville, Ill.: The Interstate Printers & Publishers, Inc., 1976.

Stadt, R.W., and B.G. Gooch. *Cooperative Education.* Indianapolis, Ind.: Bobbs-Merrill Co., 1977.

Wanat, J.A. *Cooperative Vocational Education.* Springfield, Ill.: Charles C. Thomas Publisher, 1980.

Wright, C.B. "Change in Unemployment Law Impacts Co-op." *Workplace Education* (1983), no. 5, 13.

CHAPTER 4
Insurance

As the high school industrial arts teacher goes through the office to pick up his mail, the secretary tells him that someone from the school district's insurance company will inspect his shop after school today. This is only his second year of teaching, and he has never before had his shop inspected. He suddenly finds himself feeling anxious and defensive, with questions racing through his mind.

Should he try to hide things or quickly lock up everything in the shop? Should he fix and correct anything that may seem a safety hazard? Should he participate in the inspection? Should he call attention to his safety concerns? What is the purpose of an insurance inspection, anyway? What actions might result from an inspection? What insurance do school districts normally carry, and how does it apply specifically to industrial education programs? In this chapter, we will focus on these and other questions that concern insurance and industrial education programs.

The Changing School Insurance Market

Faced with a surge in lawsuits, American schools, colleges, and universities now find they must pay significantly more than in previous years for liability insurance—if they can get it at all. According to a November 1985 AP wire-service story, insurance costs for a local school district in Arizona climbed from $117,500 for $11 million of insurance coverage to $658,000 for $6 million of coverage over a two-year period.[1] This amounts to an increase of 460 percent for a little more than half as much coverage. The Arizona school district's situation reflects a trend evident throughout the insurance industry today.

According to William H. Lilly, senior vice-president of the Fred S. James Company of Oregon, insurance companies are now responding to several years of highly unsatisfactory underwriting results. Starting in late 1984, the companies began to dramatically increase their rates. Schools and colleges did not escape this trend, and their premiums in 1985 and 1986 were often double or triple those of 1983 and 1984. Lilly notes that this problem is further exacerbated by the refusal of many insurance companies to consider insuring school risks.

Insurers blame the higher premiums, in part, on an explosion in lawsuits against schools, colleges, and universities in the last few years and on the unpredictability of court awards. This is a controversial and complex issue, involving insurance companies, lawyers, business, and public agencies. While insurers blame higher premiums on the increase in litigation, lawyers and public agencies suggest it results from poor management practices.[2] Regardless of the causes of the current liability insurance crisis, it is likely that state or federal action will either establish limits on awards and damages or increase insurance regulation.

Lawsuits are not limited to the question of liability in accidents or injuries. Especially at community colleges and universities, suits alleging sex and race discrimination in hiring and tenure decisions are among the fastest-growing areas of litigation.

According to Jerre Ward, risk manager for Michigan State University, insurance companies that cover schools, colleges, and universities are reacting to the changing insurance market by (1) reducing coverage, (2) reducing limits, and (3) raising prices. As a result, many schools now accept greater responsibility for their own insurance protection through increased self-insurance and risk management.

Although industrial educators may not find themselves directly involved in purchasing school insurance, the changing insurance market will have some impact on their programs. It will result in an even greater emphasis on safety and accident prevention programs in classes that have a high level of risk, such as industrial education, physical education, and science. Industrial education instructors who can maintain a record of accident-free class hours through a well-designed safety program will help their school district or college keep insurance premiums within reasonable bounds.

Insurance and Risk Management

The purpose of any insurance is to provide protection from potential losses. Through insurance, many school districts pay a little to assure financial protection for the large losses of a few. In instructing students, school districts or colleges build and maintain facilities, purchase equipment and supplies, and hire personnel. Each activity has varying degrees of risk. As schools become involved in activities with increased risk, they require more insurance services.

Unfortunately, the purchase of insurance by individuals and by private and public institutions is all too often a reactive process. It frequently results from an accident or the realization that certain activities could bring substantial losses. A far more positive and effective approach combines a strong insurance program with a well-thought-out risk-management program.

A risk-management program involves thorough evaluation of all potential hazards; consideration of ways to reduce or eliminate risk; and, as a last resort, transfer of risk to an insurance company. It has been well established that a professional risk-management program will reduce injuries as well as effectively protect against property and financial losses. Many school districts and colleges identify a central administrator to serve as a risk-management director. This administrator must have the support and advice of other professionals, such as insurance agents, lawyers, safety specialists, and others familiar with program operation and facilities.

The most critical aspect of risk management involves a strong safety program. A professionally designed safety program that follows the guidelines outlined in Chapter 1 can significantly limit a school district's risks by reducing both the frequency and severity of accident losses.

Types of Insurance

General Liability Insurance

Liability insurance protects a school district from the results of its negligent acts. Frequently called *third-party* coverage, it protects the school from the claims of persons not included in the insurance contract, such as students and visitors. It covers premises and operations liability; operation of automobiles, watercraft, and aircraft; and liability for products manufactured or distributed by the school district.

Liability insurance has limits for the amount of the maximum liability that can be imposed on a school. Limits range from $100,000 to $50 million depending on school district size, state laws involved, and exposure to risk.

As an example of a typical liability claim, consider the case of a student who sustained an injury while working in a school's machine shop. In addition to medical expenses of $28,000, the student suffered a permanent partial disability due to loss of four fingers on his right hand. This type of claim generally falls under the school's comprehensive general liability policy. In a case like this, the insurance company would have a responsibility to investigate the claim; talk with the injured student, his parents, or attorney; and initiate a settlement offer that reflects the facts of the accident. If the matter should go into litigation, the insurance company's attorney usually represents the teacher and others named in the lawsuit.

In claims of this type, the school, the teacher involved, and the teacher's supervisors must cooperate in every way with the insurance company, its adjusters, and its legal counsel. Before settling a claim, the insurance company will conduct a thorough investigation of the accident and all the facts related to it. The investigator will want to know if the student received proper supervision, if the teacher provided appropriate safety instruction, and if the equipment involved was properly guarded and maintained.

After an accident occurs in your class, document all pertinent facts. The prompt and consistent use of accident reports will greatly help you, your school, and your insurance company. Be completely open and honest with your insurance representative. Don't hide or misrepresent facts to make yourself look good. The school's insurance company is there to protect you and your school. Do everything you can to help.

Property Insurance

Property insurance provides protection for the loss of school-owned or controlled property, including all buildings and their contents. Policies can include coverage against specific perils such as fire, wind storm, riot, and vehicle damage. They can be broadened to insure against "all risks," subject to certain exclusions (e.g., vandalism, wear and tear, or obsolescence).

Property insurance frequently has a deductible, whose size depends on the school's ability to absorb a certain degree of loss. Deductibles of $1,000 and $5,000 are common today, but they are increasing rapidly as a result of the changing insurance market.

Property insurance can include losses contingent on unrealized profit. For example, the loss of a house that the construction class is building could also mean a loss of profits from the sale of the house. A serious fire in the student bookstore could cause loss of profits normally generated from the sale of student supplies.

A typical property insurance claim might involve a case where an explosion destroys a welding lab, leaving it a total loss for insurance purposes. The school district must establish to the satisfaction of the insurance company the exact dollar amount of the loss. If the building was not insured on a new-replacement-cost basis, the insurance company can deduct from the replacement value a depreciation that reflects the building's age and condition.

A similar process determines compensation for damaged equipment and supplies. The insurance company will request an itemized inventory, with replacement values, of all equipment and supplies. One way to maintain an accurate inventory involves taking several photographs of your shop each year and labeling them with pertinent information. The insurance company will also investigate a claim carefully for violations of policy warranties. For example, if an automatic sprinkle system in a building was turned off or if guard service warranted on an insurance policy was discontinued, the insurance company might have grounds to deny the claim or a large portion of it.

Worker's Compensation Insurance

Worker's compensation insurance protects the school district or college from claims arising from injury to employees. Like any other employer, school districts must, by law, carry worker's compensation insurance on their employees. Set by state statute, the administration and benefit structure of worker's compensation varies widely from state to state. Large school districts with vast resources may find great advantage in self-insuring this risk, but they still have a responsibility to abide by all state regulations and assure proper claims management.

A typical worker's compensation claim might involve a case where an industrial education teacher receives severe injury while using machinery in the school shop. To receive financial benefits under worker's compensation, an employee must demonstrate that (1) an accidental injury occurred, (2) it happened in or arose from the course of emploment, and (3) he or she has some temporary or permanent disability as a result of the injury.

Neither negligence on the part of the injured employee nor contributory negligence on the part of another employee is defense to most workers' compensation claims. Most workers' compensation policies provide full medical and partial disability benefits, depending on the seriousness of the injury and the time required for recovery.

Personal Insurance

In additional to insurance coverage through the school district, you may have personal insurance coverage. This is insurance coverage that you purchase, beyond that provided by your employer. You'll find personal liability insurance available at present from a variety of carriers and professional associations. Both The American Vocational Association and the International Technology Education Association make liability insurance available to members at additional cost. In the future, this coverage will very likely be difficult to get and will certainly cost more. Keep in mind that this coverage only extends to the limits identified in your policy, and that it only applies while you are within the scope and course of your employment. These policies provide secondary coverage and come into play after the primary coverage of the school district or college is exhausted. Before you purchase personal liability insurance, ask about the extent of coverage through your school district or college policy. Determine whether your school district has a deductible on its liability policy. If so, will the district pay legal expenses and possible damages that fall within the deductible? Use your personal insurance agent as a source of information.

Inspections

Your industrial education facility may be examined by a variety of inspectors for many different reasons. The most common inspections are made by fire inspectors, federal or state worker's compensation officials, the state department of education, insurance company representatives, and, in the case of self-inspection, by industrial education teachers or administrators. The local fire marshal may make a fire jurisdiction inspection on a regular or intermittent basis. The marshal can assure that you have—in good working order—the correct type of fire extinguishers. He or she may also check electrical fusing and wiring and look for proper storage of flammable materials, such as solvents or oily rags.

While not as common as inspection, your school may be checked by a representative of the federal or state worker's compensation boards. This type of inspection focuses on possible hazards to employees. Such things as proper ventilation and safe facilities and equipment would be noted.

Your state department of education may conduct a periodic evaluation and assessment that includes a safety inspection of industrial education facilities. Procedures for state department accreditation visits will vary from state to state, but safety presents an important consideration in any evaluation. The state department representative has special interest in your overall safety plan, machine guards, eye protection, storage of flammable materials, and general shop organization.

Your school district or college may have insurance from one company or several. Consequently, you may have separate inspections for liability, property, and worker's compensation insurance. Through these inspections, insurance companies can minimize risks by identifying and correcting potential problems before accidents occur. With the present volatile and changing school insurance market, the trend is toward more frequent and more careful inspections.

An insurance inspection may take place to establish a new policy and rate structure or to review existing ones. In either case an insurance inspector has special interest in overall class management and structure, eye protection, class control, class size, machine guarding, and in the teacher's attitude toward safety.

Self-inspection can offer your most valuable protection. A consistent plan for inspections that involves the teacher, administrators, and students can improve safety and provide a good learning experience for everyone. Including administrators or advisory committee members will increase the visibility of your program and emphasize the importance of safety.

You can use any of several inspection checklist forms. The AVA and the National Safety Council offer, at minimal cost, a jointly developed, easy-to-use checklist. Another valuable resource is *Standards for Technology Education Programs*, available from the International Technology Education Association.

As your school year begins, mark three or four dates on the calendar to remind yourself to conduct self-inspections. As the industrial education teacher, you are in the best position to use regular inspections to improve and document your facility's safety conditions.

Working with Your Insurance Company

As schools grow more involved in activities that have potential risk, school districts and colleges must take a more active role as consumers of insurance. An administrator in your school—often a business manager or risk-management specialist—will act as liaison with the district's insurance broker or underwriters. Most often, a school district contracts with an insurance broker to obtain the insurance services it needs. The insurance broker then communicates with insurance underwriters to obtain the different types of insurance for the school district.

School districts and colleges should carefully examine the services currently offered or needed from their insurance broker or company. This process should include input from all personnel associated with any type of risk or with activities that have been dangerous in the past. It is entirely appropriate for school districts and colleges to request a list of possible insurance services. These insurance services could include (1) maintenance of property insurance values with annual updating; (2) complete loss runs on all lines of insurance with quarterly or semiannual updating; (3) marketing reports that cover activities with various insurers; (4) annual reports summarizing the year's activity, policy changes, projections of future coverage needs, and recommendations for change; and (5) the assistance of professional staff with insurance, risk management, and safety expertise.

To supplement their insurance policies, school districts and colleges should regularly request written statements that indicate who is insured, the extent of coverage, and who will adjust any losses. For example, a school might ask whether its insurance covers a retired welder who works as an aide in several classes.

As an industrial education teacher or administrator, your contact and communications regarding insurance should go through the administrator in charge of school insurance. You stand in the best position to identify the insurance services you and your program need.

Don't fear that asking for clarification of your program's insurance status will jeopardize your safely run program. Insurance companies do not close down programs or make decisions regarding the educational program. However, if they identify dangerous and consistent hazards, they can cancel insurance coverage. They can best provide insurance coverage when they fully know the risks you need to insure.

Good industrial education programs that teach students the safe and correct use of tools and machinery benefit insurance companies. In fact, they might be considered a long-range risk-management effort because today's students are tomorrow's industrial workers. An investment in safety education today will pay future benefits.

Recommendations

Your school's insurance agent acts as a working partner in the safe operation of your industrial education program. Follow these five recommendations to build a good working relationship with your insurance agent and to provide a safe environment for yourself and your students:

● Stress safety in your curriculum.

● Consider your insurance agent a working partner. Recognize the importance of honesty and candor when working with your insurance agent or underwriter.

● Conduct regular safety inspections of facilities and equipment.

● Maintain accurate inventories of all major equipment and supplies.

● Keep your administrator or risk-management director informed of the insurance services you need.

References

[1]Bayles, F. "The Insurance Drought." *The Coravllis Gazette Times,* 24 November 1985, D1.

[2]"The Manufactured Crisis." *Consumer Reports,* August 1986, 544-49.

Resources

Devine, R. J. "Only You Can Take the Mystery Out of Risk Management and Protect Your Schools." *The American School Board Journal* 169 (1982), no. 9, 33-35.

Hester, D. A. "In a Quandary? The Time to Formulate a Purchasing Plan is Before You Spec Insurance." *American School and University* 56 (1983), no. 4, 28-29.

Sherman, J.M. "Risk Management: Do You Understand Your Insurance Program?" *American School and University* 57 (1985), no. 8, 61-63.

CHAPTER 5

Writing Student Recommendations

A technical college instructor receives a phone call from a local building contractor who asks about a student in the construction class. The contractor has just read the instructor's written recommendation of the student and wants more information. The instructor is glad the contractor is calling because when she wrote the recommendation she hesitated to mention that the student caused trouble in class and almost always completed his assignments late. Except for these behavior problems, he has been one of the most talented and capable students. When the contractor asks about the student's work and social skills, the instructor feels free to describe the behaviors she didn't mention in the written recommendation.

Why do so many of us fear *writing* something about someone when we wouldn't worry about *saying* the same thing? Do we fear a lawsuit for defamation of character? Do we think it harder to prove a verbal statement to a jury than a written one? Do we lack confidence in our ability to write a good letter of recommendation?

All industrial education teachers know that part of their responsibility involves providing employers and colleges with information about students' behavior and achievements. In this chapter, we will review many legal questions industrial education teachers face when they give written and verbal recommendations. We'll also provide practical suggestions for giving recommendations that will meet the needs of employers and college officials while protecting the confidentiality of the student-teacher relationship.

Defamation of Character

First, we examine the student's right not be be defamed. Defamation consists of the twin torts of libel and slander. Defamatory communication in written or printed form is called libel; in spoken form, slander. In either form, defamation involves an invasion of interests in reputation and good name. It diminishes the esteem and respect in which another person is held, or it incites adverse, derogatory, or unpleasant feelings or opinions against another. To prove defamation, the plaintiff must establish that (1) the words in question are actionable, (2) the words refer to the plaintiff, (3) the words are defamatory in ther ordinary and normal meaning and in the context, and (4) the defamation was communicated.

Defamation can be committed indirectly, or by inuendo, if the words in question can impugn a defamatory charge in a particular context. A person who republishes or repeats a defamatory statement made by another can also be guilty of the tort of libel or slander. In summary, defamation requires unprivileged communication to a third person of a false or misleading statement that damages the victim's reputation, whether the communication is made intentionally or negligently.

Remember, though, that not every criticism is defamatory and truth of the statement always provides a defense. In addition, a number of legal doctrines protect the professional educator from liability should a student decide to sue. The most important involves the doctrine of qualified privilege, which recognizes the importance of honest and candid communication among professionals in the ordinary course of public business. Our society considers the communication of pertinent and accurate information more important than the supression or alteration of facts for fear of retaliation.

The Doctrine of Qualified Privilege

The doctrine of qualified privilege encourages freedom of discussion by public officials where such freedom is necessary to the conduct of public business. For example, consider the communications between the teacher and employer described in the anecdote that starts this chapter. As long as remarks relate to the school's legitimate business and are not made maliciously, a teacher is immune from liability for statements made in a professional conversation *even though the statements may be proven untrue and damaging to the student's character and reputation*. The doctrine of qualified privilege applies when communication of certain information is reasonably necessary for the protection of one's own, a third party's, or the public's interest.

In other words, public school teachers and administrators have a legal privilege to communicate any statement, written or spoken, about any other person to a third party without fear of liability as long as the statement is (1) necessary to the conduct of public business and (2) not malicious and communicated in good faith. Malice is legally defined as a wrongful act committed intentionally or with evil intent and without just cause or excuse. It does not necessarily imply spite against any individual but in many instances merely a wanton disposition, grossly negligent of the rights of others. The doctrine of qualified privilege protects even a false statement written or spoken in good faith and reasonably believed to be true.

As a general rule, potentially defamatory information should be communicated only to someone who has a legitimate interest in and stands in a position to act on that information. Note that the teacher-pupil relationship imposes a *higher standard of conduct* on the teacher than would exist if the two parties dealt with one another as equals. Consequenlty, a teacher must exhibit good faith in discharging a duty to a pupil. Good faith, as defined by the courts, requires that the teacher refrain from taking advantage of the pupil; act honestly, with good motives and intent, and without fraud, collusion, or deceit; and make a concerted effort to determine and act upon the truth in any matter involving a pupil. Disclosure of defamatory information concerning a pupil is made in good faith *only* if made to a person to whom the teacher must, as a duty, disclose the information—such as a principal—or if made to someone professionally qualified to assist the pupil—such as counselor, college official, or prospective employer. Good faith requires that communication regarding rumors or suspicions about pupil occur only with a person to whom the teacher has a positive duty to report such information.

Writing and Talking about Students

We now have a sense of how the law defines defamation and the protection afforded educators by the doctrine of qualified privilege. How can we apply this information to daily activities?

Don't use labels. Labels can hide and obscure your meaning, leading to a misunderstanding of your statement. In place of labels, use statements that describe, detail, narrate, illustrate, or characterize a student's behavior and achievements.

For example, a statement like "Herbie has sticky fingers" may have more than one meaning. Instead of using a label, you should describe Herbie's behavior with descriptive statements and firsthand information. You might say, "Every day we have cinnamon rolls at lunch, Herbie comes to class with sticky fingers. As a result, he gets all the tools and machines sticky." Or say, "I have caught Herbie a number of times trying to steal tools from the school shop." "Sticky fingers" is a common label for identifying students who steal and students whose fingers are covered with something sticky. However, the difference to a prospective employer between a thief and a sloppy eater is great—one you would not hire because he isn't trustworthy and the other you would hire but perhaps not ask out to lunch! What a difference describing behavior makes to an employer looking for the best person for a job!

Consider the statement: "Susie is lazy." Does this mean she sleeps in class, does not hand in work on time, shows up late, daydreams, demonstrates a lack of interest in projects, or does not assume leadership roles? On the other hand, does it mean that Susie has a learning disability not yet diagnosed? If a teacher thinks in terms of describing firsthand experiences with a student and lets the third party decide on a label, he or she not only passes along better information but, legally speaking, stands on much safer ground. If Susie alleges some day that your label of "lazy" was a detriment to her getting a job, you'll find it far easier to prove that Susie was late for class than to remember and provide enough examples of her behavior to convince a court that she should be labeled "lazy."

Making Recommendations

Some specific strategies may help in writing letters of recommendation or talking with a third party about one of your industrial education students. Whether your recommendation is written or spoken, it must be accurate, organized, and relevant to the decision your reader or listener must make.

Recommendations usually go to a prospective employer or an

educational program. Although both seek similar information about applicants, most employers look for specific information related to on-the-job performance, while educators want to know about a student's academic ability. In considering what to discuss, put yourself in the position of the person making a decision based on the information you will provide.

Ask students seeking a written recommendation to give you a copy of their resume and a statement of their career goals. A personal conference with the student helps to clarify your analysis of the student's abilities and gives the student some idea of what your recommendation will be. A student will be at great disadvantage in an interview without some notion of the substance of your recommendation. You might also use the conference to help a student who has an unrealistic self-concept or to reinforce one who has goals that fit personal interest and abilities. In most cases, a teacher can provide the most objective and complete assessment of a student to *both* the student and an interested employer or educational institution.

Legal access by teachers to students' official school records varies from state to state, and even within some states. In any case, use caution when including information gathered from this source. Most information contained in school records is intended for educational purposes only. Much of that included years ago may no longer be relevant or accurate. You can safely use directory information, such as home address, telephone number, class standing (not grade point average), participation in school activities, dates of attendance, awards, and names of schools previously attended. Consider all other information confidential. In addition, students may request holding confidential *all* information, including directory information. In this case, the student's record should contain a notice to this effect.

The Family Rights and Privacy Act allows students and/or their parents access to all educational information concerning the student. If you retain a copy of a letter you write, consider it an educational record and accessible to the student. Keep this in mind if you want to write a confidential letter of recommendation. Instructors who save old recommendations for use as models in writing new ones need only mark out the student's name to insure confidentially.

Writing the Letter

Ideally, you should direct your letter to the person seeking the information. "To whom it may conern," your second-best option, is, however, far better than providing nothing in writing for a student earnestly seeking a job. Often, a student will have numerous interviews for the same type of work and in this case, as a convenience to you, one letter of general reference should prove acceptable. Consider the guidelines that follow.

● *First paragraph*—Keep it short and to the point. State your reason for writing the letter, the student's name, and how long and in what context you have known him or her. The first paragraph introduces you, sets your frame of reference, and lets the reader know how much weight to put on information that will follow. Two to four sentences should suffice, depending on how well you know the student.

● *Second paragraph*—By far the most important part of the recommendation, this section gives the reader the most significant information for making a decision about the candidate. The second paragraph should provide firsthand examples in the form of statements that describe the student's abilities and personal characteristics. Prospective employers and educators have special interest in the following topics: (1) knowledge of technical subject matter and ability to apply that knowledge on the job, (2) ability to learn new skills and work in different situations, (3) written and oral communication skills, (4) management skills and the ability to work independently, accept responsibility, and get the job done, (5) interpersonal relationships and the ability to be flexible, adaptable, and work effectively with other people, (6) personal worth and integrity and the presence of such traits as self-confidence, reliability, punctuality, poise, and enthusiasm, and (7) academic ability.

Many recommendations seem written out of a sense of duty and show little life or creativity to attract the readers' interest and attention. Add some zest to your recommendations. Anecdotes or short narratives about the student add originality and genuineness to your recommendation. If you are truly enthusiastic about a student, let it show. Throw in a "Bravo!" or a "Wow! What a worker!" Keep in mind, though, that too much of this, will detract from the essence of your letter. Obviously, the second paragraph may easily expand into two or more paragraphs, depending on how well you know the student or the employer. Take your time writing this part of the letter, and include as much relevant information as possible.

● *Third paragraph*—In your closing paragraph, summarize your recommendation in clear, succinct terms. Here, you might also re-state the student's career plans and their relationship to the job sought. Include your telephone number and encourage a call for more information. If you yourself would hire the student, explain why. If you're not certain, don't mention it. If you cannot recommend the student, you should not be writing a recommendation and should have told the student that.

End with a positive statement that describes how you feel about the student and the predictability of his or her success on the job. Including your address and phone number below your signature lets the reader know that you're accessible and available for more information and clarification.

Don't think you must limit your recommendation to one page because that's all an employer will read. If you have two or more pages of good information, let that determine the length of your letter. Employers seeking good employees are delighted to have two pages of information about an applicant. Most employers look for good reasons to hire a person and a well-written, comprehensive, firsthand account of a student's performance should have no predetermined boundaries.

Your recommendation should be free of grammatical error, neatly typed, and on letterhead stationery. You might ask your secretary or a student office aide for typing help. Be sure, though, to proofread anything typed for you. Good first impressions and the letter's appearance are important reflections of the integrity and credibility of its content.

Recommendation Forms

On occasion the classroom teacher must complete a recommendation form that requests specific information pertinent to the abilities and responsibilities required for a particular job. Many of these forms include a list of applicant abilities and characteristics followed by a scale with directions to check the appropriate number or point along the given continuum. Although checklists of this type may provide little factual information about the student, they serve as a worthwhile guideline for information an employer or college official needs. A checklist also serves as a valuable quick review and first-impression statement about the written recommendation that follows.

An employer or school official may also use a standard recommendation form to compare students from different schools or colleges. As you mark the appropriate number or place on the continuum, you must make sure that you have thought through the reasons for your decision and have carefully considered your message. If there is a place for a narrative statement near the item listed, take time to write something about the reason for the placement of your check. This short narrative statement adds far greater weight and substance to your opinion than a simple check mark following a statement on a form.

Most checklists are followed by a space for a narrative statement about the student. Your comments here should flesh out the items enumerated in the checklist. If you marked the student low on one item, provide a reason for it in the narrative statement. Do the same, of course, for very high marks. The reader in this case wants more information about and examples of the outstanding work and achievements of your student. Anyone using this type of recommendation form will be frustrated by a teacher who marks a student low in an area, then writes about other things in the narrative section and never mentions the reasons for the low mark. A well-written narrative statement is indispensable to a checklist recommendation. It will help the employer or school make a good decision and serves as flesh to fill out the bones the recommendation form provides.

In some instances, letterhead stationery helps the student more than a recommendation form provided by an employer, college, or placement office. If your school has a reputation of excellence and its graduates are highly recruited, letterhead stationery adds clout and ambience that a recommendation form cannot convey. Although you give up the specific information and organization of a checklist, the flag and colors of your school may more than compensate. The form you receive from the student, however, can serve as an outline for the contents of a narrative statement written on letterhead stationery. Consider this option when you are asked to complete a recommendation form.

Recommendations for Placement Files

Lately, more and more vocational education programs provide placement services for their graduates. One problem common to all placement activities is the question of who owns the recommendation and who controls the student's placement file. In almost every case, placement files used for job and school placement are initiated by the student seeking a position. Here, the contents of that file should belong to the student. The institution assumes the role of custodian of the placement file and has a duty to maintain the file for its intended purposes. Those who write recommendations contained in the placement file usually retain ownership of the contents of what they have written. Although rules vary somewhat, this view is considered best and preferred by the majority of placement offices that maintain files for their students.

Two questions arise regarding the use and control of the student's recommendation after the placement office receives it. First, can the student legally request the removal of a recommendation from his or her placement file? Most placement offices permit this practice because the student initiated the file and usually chooses the persons who write the recommendations. If the student can decide whether or not to have a file and choose who writes the recommendations, then the student should have control over the material in the file. This includes having authority to destroy the complete file if so desired. On the other hand, students cannot control files that are school initiated, such as transcripts and health records.

Second, can the author of a recommendation change or retract it once it is received by a placement office for inclusion in a student's placement file? This may occur when the writer of a recommendation discovers additional information about the student that makes the recommendation no longer an accurate statement of the writer's opinion. If a recommendation represents a candid opinion of the person who wrote it, that person should be allowed to change the statement to correspond with his or her recent opinion. Not allowing writers to change their statements once submitted to the office could result in offending some employers and school staff, which could in turn lead to an uncooperative attitude regarding the writing of further letters for placement files and to a diminished credibility for all placement file recommendations. For these reasons, the contents of the recommendation should belong to the writer, the contents of the placement file to the student, and the care and maintenance of the file itself to the placement office.

Confidentiality

The Family Rights and Privacy Act of 1974 states:

> An individual who is an applicant for admission to an institution of postsecondary education or is a student in attendance at an institution of postsecondary education may waive his or her right to inspect and review confidential letters and confidential statements of recommendation except that the waiver may apply to confidential letters and statements only if: (1) The applicant or student is, upon request, notified of the names of all individuals providing the letters or statements; (2) the letters or statements are used only for the purpose for which they were originally intended, and (3) such waiver is not required by the agency or institution as a condition of admission to or receipt of any other service or benefit from the agency or institution.[1]

Unless a student has waived the right to review a recommendation, he or she as a right to access to all educational records. Most recommendation forms contain a waiver statement that if signed by the student, assures the writer of the recommendation that it will not be reviewed by the student. If the statement is unsigned, the recommendation is considered open to the student's review under the Family Rights and Privacy Act. If the student revokes this waiver, the recommendation made in confidence remains confidential and only statements made subsequent to the revocation of waiver are open to the student. The student must make any revocation in writing.

Students often inquire about the advisability of having open versus confidential letters of recommendation. Arguments for confidentiality rest on the premise that it allows the person making the recommendation to be more candid and forthright and, therefore, gives more integrity and weight to the recommendation. Most of us would agree that it is easier to make statements about an applicant who is not present than to say the same things, good or bad, to a third person about an applicant sitting next to you. Reasons for having an open recommendation range from mistrust of the writer to the fact that it offers the applicant knowledge of what kind of topics to talk about in a related interview. Good points lie on both sides, and time should be spent helping the student make the best choice for his or her situation.

In summary, do not fear the law when talking or writing about students. Qualified privilege provides teachers more than enough legal protection for candid, straightforward, and truthful communication among professionals. If a student has done poorly in your class, you have a professional responsibility to pass that information on to a prospective employer.

Do not use labels. Use statements that describe and characterize students' behavior and achievements and let the readers choose a label if they wish. Do not feel forced to write a standard or form recommendation. Let your personal enthusiasm show in your letter. Finally, take the time from your busy schedule to write letters of recommendation worthy and befitting you, the program you represent, and the student whose future will be affected by your recommendation.

Reference

[1]Family Educational Rights and Privacy Act of 1974, P.L. 93-380, Section 99.7 (c).

Resources

Bolles, Richard Nelson. *What Color is Your Parachute?* Berkeley, Calif.: Ten Speed Press, 1985.

Medley, H. Anthony. *Sweaty Palms: The Neglected Art of Being Interviewed.* Berkeley, Calif.: Ten Speed Press, 1984.

Jackson, Tom. *Guerilla Tactics in the Job Market.* New York: Bantam Books, 1978.

Jones, Ilene. *Jobs for Teenagers.* New York: Ballantine Books, 1983.

Half, Robert. *Robert Half on Hiring.* New York: Crown Publishers, 1985.

Holms, Max. *Writing Your College Application and Essay.* New York: Monarch Press, 1984.

CHAPTER 6

Eliminating Sex Stereotyping

Imagine yourself the owner of an auto repair shop. You are proud and pleased when your daughter begins working in your shop after school. When you first invited her, she was hesitant, but now she has started asking the mechanics questions and shows a real interest in the work. When it comes time for her to register for high school classes, you're not surprised to find that she wants to sign up for Introductory Auto Mechanics. You are later very upset to hear that the school counselor says she can't enroll in the class because it's for "boys only."

You have for years donated parts to the school's industrial education program and had served on its advisory committee, but you had no idea girls were discouraged from taking the automotive class. When you call the teacher to discuss the problem, he says it has been his experience that girls generally don't like to crawl under cars or get their hands dirty, and beside that there is only one washroom in the shop area. In other words, who ever heard of a girl who was serious about mechanics? Some of what he says seems to make sense—in fact, you have said similar things yourself in the past. But when it comes time to discuss the situation with your own daughter, you know there must be something wrong with the system.

This incident, which may have been common in the past, occurs less often today. Our beliefs in sex stereotypes have changed profoundly and this has an impact on all aspects of society, including home, school, and work. Women and men alike increasingly recognize and explore new options.

In considering this issue, we must first distinguish between sex discrimination and sex bias. Sex discrimination is generally regarded as illegal behavior that denies someone's legal rights or limits his or her future opportunities. An industrial education program that focuses only on legal compliance usually produces defensiveness and resentment among its participants. Few people consciously discriminate, and many resent the government telling them what to do and not to do in their classroom.

Bias, on the other hand, is a personally meaningful system of assumptions and feelings one experiences from birth that serves as a pattern or guide for understanding events and the actions of others. A bias, for example, could be the belief that women and men are and should be different, not only physically, but in personality, ability, and strength and that, therefore, they should hold different occupations. We do not intend to decide here what is good or bad sex bias but to delineate it from sex discrimination and treat it as a separate and, in many ways, more important issue. The law itself is fairly clear and direct—it simply prohibits discrimination on the basis of sex. But, to understand the many ways discriminatory practices and actions manifest themselves in our daily lives necessitates a genuine awareness and sensitivity to those "left out" or harrassed because of their sex. This chapter will examine the laws on sex discrimination and some examples of teacher and administrative behavior that violates their spirit.

Relevant Legislation

Several pieces of legislation enacted in the past decade have helped bring about dramatic and far-reaching changes in the area of sex discrimination. Title IX of the Education Amendments of 1972 prohibits discrimination on the basis of sex against students and employees of schools receiving federal financial assistance. Title VII of the Civil Rights Act of 1964 prohibits discrimination against employees on the basis of race, color, national origin, religion, or sex by any employer in the United States who employs 15 or more people.

The Equal Pay Act as amended in 1972 prohibits discrimination on the basis of sex in wages and fringe benefits by any employer in the United States. The Vocational Education Act of 1963, as amended by the Education Amendments of 1976, P.L. 94-482, requires states to make new efforts to overcome sex discrimination and sex stereotyping in vocational education. The most recent vocational education legislation, the Carl Perkins Vocational Education Act of 1984, P.L. 98-524, requires vocational education programs to actively address issues related to sex stereotyping. The Carl Perkins Act requires that every state assign one individual to administer vocational education programs that will expand vocational education opportunities for women. The Act also mandates that each state spend at least $60,000 annually to carry out the activities of personnel assigned to eliminate sex discrimination and sex stereotyping. As a result of this new legislation, there will be both personnel and resources available to industrial educators to eliminate sex discrimination and sex stereotyping as it relates to their programs.

The Rules and Regulations for P.L. 98-524 as presented in Section 401.56 of the Federal Register identify how funds from the Carl Perkins Act may be used to eliminate sex bias and stereotyping in vocational education:

> (a) A State shall use funds reserved for individuals who participate in programs designed to eliminate sex bias and stereotyping in vocational education in accordance with §401.92(e) for
>> (1) Programs, services, and activities to eliminate sex bias and stereotyping in secondary and postsecondary vocational education programs;
>> (2) vocational education programs, services, and activities for girls and women aged 14 through 25, designed to enable the participants to support themselves and their familes; and
>> (3) support services for individuals participating in vocational education programs, services, and activities described in paragraphs (a) (1) and (a) (2) of this section, including dependent-care services and transportation.
>
> (b) A State may waive the age limitations in paragraph (a)(2) of this section if the person described in §401.13(a) determines that the waiver is essential to meet the objectives of this section.[1]

In addition, most states have enacted legislation prohibiting unreasonably different treatment of students or employees in any public school program that receives state funds.

Legislation by itself cannot eliminate sex discrimination. To help insure equal opportunity regardless of sex, classroom teachers must clearly understand how the laws affect their programs. Most of us resist change and are reluctant to take seriously or enforce a law that does not match our personal biases. We all have strong stereotypic images of men and women based on our experiences and our environment. We do not suggest that every teacher must erase his or her stereotypes completely, even if that were possible, but instead that all of us in education have a responsibility to insure that all our students have equal opportunity to educational offerings regardless of sex.

Remedying Sex Discrimination

Remedial and Affirmative Action

The landmark legislation concerning sex discrimination appears in Title IX of the Education Amendments of 1972. Its regulations cover two major provisions: remedial action (Section 86.3(a)) and affirmative action (Section 86.3(b)).

Remedial action indicates that a rule or policy in an educational program or activity that has a discriminatory effect must be changed to eliminate the discrimination. For example, in our opening anecdote, remedial action would simply require eliminating the "boys only" policy, thus opening the class to both boys and girls.

Affirmative action requires a school to take further measures to compensate for previous discrimation and make every effort to encourage participation by students whose opportunities have previously been limited. For example, instructors can place posters around the school announcing that auto mechanics is now open to both boys and girls. The school newspaper might do a feature story on a woman mechanic in the area or about someone like Shirley Muldowney, a world champion top fuel eliminator. Counselors and teachers could encourage girls to consider auto mechanics.

Sex stereotyping and discrimination is a sensitive issue. Teachers should consider their individual students' feelings and avoid potentially embarrassing or intimidating situations. Instead of having one girl come into auto mechanics class alone on the first day, why not try to have several? If there is only one washroom in the industrial education area, make clear arrangements for both boys and girls. A teacher's saying, "Watch your language, boys, we now have girls in the class," would be embarrassing and simply not equal treatment or opportunity for the girls in the class. Awareness of stereotyping actions and statements is essential to affirmative action.

The Compliance Officer

Section 86.8 of Title IX requires each school district to designate at least one employee to coordinate its efforts to comply with and carry out responsibilities under the law. This includes investigation of any complaint of noncompliance or discrimination. The school district must notify all students and employees of the name, office address, and telephone number of the school district's Title IX compliance officer. In addition, the school district must adopt and publish grievance procedures that provide for prompt and equitable resolution of student and employee complaints that allege any action prohibited by Title IX.

Unfortunately, in many school districts the compliance officer is not well known. In most cases, he or she is an administrator who serves as affirmative action officer along with other assigned responsibilities. The school district's central office can tell you that individual's name. Note that this person is available to *both* students and employees.

The responsibility of the Title IX compliance officer is not to take sides in a complaint but to advise students or employees of their rights under the law and to provide assistance through the grievance process. An effective compliance officer can help resolve complaints of discrimination before they evolve into grievance proceedings.

Title IX identifies nine subject areas within the school that require special attention and evaluation: health, physical, business, music, adult, home-economics, industrial, vocational, and technical education. These areas are identified as ones where different treatment, denial, or limitation of students will most likely occur due to course-offering imbalances, course access, or a faculty-student interaction imbalance.

Course-Offering Imbalance

Industrial education offerings, like all other course offerings, must be open to all students regardless of sex, age, handicap, national origin, race, marital status, or religion. An imbalance in student enrollment is one indication of sex discrimination. If an industrial education class shows a 90 percent male enrollment when the overall school enrollment is 50 percent male and 50 percent female, the school must evaluate the reasons for the imbalance. It must determine whether there has been sponsored action that discourages female enrollment. If the school discovers any past discouragement or discrimination by a teacher or counselor, as in our example with the automotive teacher, the school must take immediate remedial and affirmative action.

Course Access and Differential Treatment

A significant lack of females in industrial education classes may result from various factors, such as a teacher's reputation for disliking having girls in a class, a counselor discouraging enrollment, or student perceptions. For example, a counselor may advise a girl not to enroll in a construction class because the counselor thinks she will later have difficulty getting related employment. This violates the law prohibiting sex discrimination in access to courses. The counselor's advice is based on a personal perception of the influence of sex in the job market. That advice constitutes differential treatment based on sex in counseling a student. A student's sex may not be a factor in making recommendations or determining eligibility for a course or program.

A teacher's reputation for treating students differently in class based on sex may also affect course access. A teacher who consistently treats females differently violates the law. The school is responsible for "significantly assisting" a teacher who treats students differently on the basis of sex and, in so doing, denies some access to courses.

Faculty-Student Interaction Imbalance

Faculty-student interaction imbalance proves harder to recognize. Considering the invisible and the very visible students provides the clearest examples. If a teacher ignores or fails to recognize girls, the girls become invisible in the class and may lose their opportunity for class participation. Also, the teacher's attitude may transfer to other students. On the other hand, if a teacher makes a student overly visible because of her sex by giving constant attention and assistance, the teacher may reinforce stereotypes. It is very difficult to draw a clear line between supportive and patronizing teacher behavior, but educators must recognize that the extremes violate the law and can damage our students.

Changes in attitudes and perceptions related to sex bias and discrimination are difficult to measure, both in ourselves and others. Ask yourself the following questions to determine whether your industrial education programs are free of sex bias or sex discrimination. They are summarized from Project MOVE materials, produced by the College of Technology, State University of New York at Utica.

1. Do you provide the same course content for students of both sexes?

2. Do you provide the same learning activities and projects for all students, rather than different ones based on sex (e.g., more labs for boys, more seat work for girls)?

3. Do you set the same standards of behavior for all students in your classroom (e.g., regarding paying attention, being quiet, talking to others)?

4. Do you apply the same standards for use of tools and equipment to all students?

5. Do you encourage all students to show consideration and courtesy to others, rather than asking that the boys be "chivalrous" and girls "ladylike"?

6. Do you apply the same standards and administer the same reprimands or disciplinary actions any student who misbehaves?

7. Do you avoid comparing boys with girls, or girls with boys in respect to classroom behavior, attitudes, and accomplishments (e.g., saying, "The girls in this class are setting an excellent example.")?

8. Do you use gender-free terms and occupational titles such as "human" and "salesclerk" instead of "mankind" and "saleslady"?

9. Do you avoid stereotyped phrases such as "boys will be boys" and "girls should act ladylike"?

10. Do you give equal attention to students of both sexes, rather than more support to girls, more criticism to boys, and so forth?

11. Do you establish the same dress code for all students (e.g., having students wearing coveralls?

12. Do you establish and apply the same grading system to students of both sexes, not making allowances for one sex to be less capable and, therefore, have work graded differently?

Our gender role expectations are so firmly ingrained that we often do not realize when we reinforce sex bias or discrimination. Industrial educators are in an excellent position to help students overcome traditional gender roles or barriers. Use the questions above to review your gender-related teaching style.

Sexual Harassment

The Equal Employment Opportunity Commission has only recently recognized and acted upon sexual harassment as a violation of Title VII of the Civil Rights Act of 1964. The Commission, on April 11, 1980, published guidelines governing this aspect of sex discrimination. Under the guidelines, unwelcome sexual advances, requests for sexual favors, and other verbal or physical conduct of a sexual nature constitute sexual harassment when: (1) submission to such conduct is made either explicitly or implicitly a term or condition of an individual's employment, (2) submission to or rejection of such conduct by an individual forms the basis for employment decisions affecting the individual, or (3) such conduct has the purpose or effect of substantially interfering with an individual's work performance or of creating an intimidating, hostile, or offensive work environment.[2]

An employer is responsible for the actions of its supervisors regardless of whether the specific acts complained of were unauthorized or even forbidden by the employer and regardless of whether the employer knew or should have known of their occurrence. Regarding harassment among nonsupervisory personnel, an employer holds responsibility when it knows or should have known of the conduct. However, an employer may rebut apparent liability for such acts by showing that it took immediate and appropriate corrective action. Not only must employers take affirmative action to prevent supervisors from harassing subordinates, they must also concern themselves about co-workers harassing one another. Some examples that *may* constitute sexual harassment are:
- subtle pressure for sexual interaction,
- repeated unnecessary brushes or touches,
- disparaging remarks about a person's gender,
- physical aggression such as pinching and patting,
- sexual innuendos made at inappropriate times,
- verbal sexual abuse disguised as humor,
- obscene gestures, or

● repeated references to various parts of the body.

Students also may be the victims or perpetrators of sexual harassment. As in employment cases, discrimination will be held to exist where a student, because of his or her sex, is subjected to demands or conditions that are not imposed on members of the opposite sex. For example, where male students in a shop course subject a female student to sexual comments, propositions, and touching, sex discrimination has occurred since the female student is subjected to conditions because of her sex to which males are not subjected. Pupils will usually take offense at the same conditions that offend adult employees, including pictures of nudes, comments and jokes, sexual advances, and requests for sexual favors. In addition, there may be some conduct that would intimidate a student that an adult would not find offensive.

To constitute a violation of Title IX, sexual harassment of a pupil must adversely affect the learning environment. It is not necessary that the pupil actually suffer a reduction of grade or withdraw from a class. It is sufficient that the pupil's psychological or emotional learning environment is adversely affected.

For a violation of Title IX to occur, the harassment must be performed by someone under the control of the school district. It is clear that teachers and other employees function under the control of the district, particularly in their relationship to pupils. Moreover, a court would also hold that a classroom teacher, and therefore the school district, is, or should be, in control of other pupils regarding maintenance of an appropriate learning environment. Schools have an obligation to control students' conduct while they pass through the halls between classes, in classrooms and cafeterias, and at school-sponsored activities. While a school district is not liable for every act done to a pupil by another pupil, a teacher, and therefore the district, has a responsibility to be aware of conduct by pupils that adversely affects the learning environment of others. Since private conduct of pupils lies within the control of a teacher to a greater degree than the private conduct of an adult co-worker, the school has a higher duty to control such conduct. Furthermore, the relationship between a student and an educational institution is different in many important respects from the relationship of an employee to an employer (e.g., the student actively *purchases* education by payment of tuition and fees or is *forced* to attend school because of the state's compulsory attendance laws). Arguably, then, the educational institution's obligation to provide a learning climate free of such distractions as sexual harassment is greater than that of an employer and supports a more comprehensive definition of discriminatory sexual harassment.

The school *must* take prompt and appropriate remedial action when it knows or should know of discriminatory harassment. Where a teacher knows that a pupil is being harassed and fails to take steps to improve the learning environment, the school district is liable under Title IX for condoning the harassment. Requests by female students to transfer from male-dominated classes should put counselors on notice that a harassment problem may exist. Counselors should have clear instructions on how to deal with such situations. The school certainly must have a procedure for investigating complaints of harassment and other forms of discrimination. Where previous harassment has existed, whether perpetrated by staff members or students, an affirmative action program is called for to remedy the present effects of such past practices.

More commonly, however, the school lacks awareness of or chooses to ignore sexual comments and advances by students directed toward other students. But whether it is females harassing a male who enrolls in a class in cooking or home economics or males harassing females who enroll in a traditionally male industrial education course, the result is the same. It breaks down the district's efforts to eliminate perpetuation of sex-biased stereotypes and frustrates the school's basic mission of assisting every student in achieving his or her personal and occupational potential. Moreover, it subjects the district to legal liability under federal and state law.

The protective attitude of the courts toward children is reflected in a consistent pattern of decisions that uphold the dismissal of elementary and secondary school teachers who become sexually involved with their pupils or other minors. This pattern extends back to a time when the courts permitted the discharge of teachers for any behavior setting an improper example for pupils. Today, the courts of most jurisdictions sustain dismissals for immoral conduct only when the evidence establishes a link between given conduct and the teacher's fitness to teach. Nonetheless, for dismissal based on sexual involvement with pupils, the courts do not require that school boards, hearing officers, or panels provide specific findings of adverse effect.

To justify the teacher's discharge, school officials need only prove that the conduct occurred.

We have a legal, social, and professional obligation to provide equal access to industrial education to all students regardless of sex. This issue holds equal importance in both industrial arts and vocational-industrial programs. As a part of general education, industrial arts should help all students learn about our industry and technology. We cannot assume that only boys will benefit from industrial education programs or that boys will make better use of their industrial education learning experiences.

In helping students choose and prepare for a future vocation, we cannot direct women toward occupations traditionally identified as "female." Even if women eventually choose to pursue traditionally "female" occupations, they should have opportunity to explore and prepare for any career of their choice.

Effective remedial and affirmative action in response to sex discrimination is not only good legal practice but is also instrumental in building class enrollment and increasing industrial education opportunities for all students.

References

[1] *Federal Register* 50 (16 August 1985), 159.

[2] Equal Employment Opportunity Commission. *Equal Employment Opportunity Commission Guidelines on Sexual Harrassment.* Section 160.11. Washington, D.C.: Equal Employment Opportunity Commission, 1980.

Resources

American Vocational Association. "Special Issue: Women in Vocational Education." *Vocational Education Journal* 60 (1985), no. 7.

Boben, Donna K., and Willis E. Ray. "Sex Equity in Industrial Arts." *Man, Society, Technology* 41 (1982), no. 4, 10-12.

Crocker, Phyllis L. "Annotated Bibliography on Sexual Harassment in Education." *Women's Rights Law Reporter* 7 (1982), no. 2 (published by Rutgers Law School, New Brunswick, N.J.).

National Education Association. *Sex Role Stereotyping in the Schools.* Washington, D.C.: National Education Association, 1977.

Till, Frank J. *Sexual Harassment: A Report on the Sexual Harassment of Students.* Washington, D.C.: National Advisory Council on Women's Educational Programs, 1980.

Weiner, Elizabeth, ed. *Sex Role Stereotyping in the Schools.* Washington, D.C.: National Education Association, 1980.

Smith, Amanda J., and Charlotte J. Farris. *Pioneering Programs in Sex Equity: A Teacher's Guide.* Washington, D.C.: American Vocational Association, 1982.

CHAPTER 7

Disadvantaged Students

In reviewing the second semester class list, the junior high industrial arts teacher notices the absence of Paul's name. He had enjoyed having Paul in the introductory industrial arts class for seventh graders and had hoped he'd enroll in this semester's elective class. The teacher is surprised he hasn't, because Paul had shown real talent for woodworking and great enthusiasm for all class activities.

The following day, the teacher encounters Paul in the hall and asks about his loss of interest in industrial arts. Paul's reply is evasive—having something to do with his maybe wanting to try choir or art. His hesitant speech and lack of eye contact make the teacher suspect there is more here than Paul is willing to share. The teacher seeks out the school counselor who helped Paul with his schedule for a fuller explanation.

The counselor explains that Paul acted very upset about dropping industrial arts, but that his mother has just lost her job and Paul wants to do his part to help his single-parent, immigrant family through its financial crisis. Paul feels he can't ask his mom for the $15 needed for the industrial arts shop ticket.

Paul is a disadvantaged student, part of a growing segment of our student population. In addition to not having the support of two parents and needing to learn a new language in school, Paul is economically disadvantaged. His situation, as described above, could not legally happen in many schools today because of federal legislation designed to help disadvantaged students and state laws that prohibit charging fees for required educational programs.

Who are disadvantaged students? How can we identify them? What are our legal responsibilities to them? How can industrial education programs help disadvantaged students? What specific strategies can we use in industrial education classes to work with disadvantaged students? This chapter will address these and other related questions.

Federal Law

Since the early 1960s, the federal government has taken an aggressive role in supporting vocational education for disadvantaged students. The Vocational Education Act of 1963 represents the first federal legislation to deal explicitly with disadvantaged students in traditional vocational programs. This act authorized funding for both disadvantaged and handicapped students. The subsequent amendments of 1968 and 1976 expanded vocational education's role in meeting the needs of disadvantaged students and increased federal funding available for this purpose.

The Carl D. Perkins Vocational Education Act of 1984 continues to expand the mission of vocational education in meeting the needs of disadvantaged students. Under the new law, states must spend 57 percent of basic grants to meet the needs of underserved students, especially the disadvantaged, the handicapped, men and women entering nontraditional occupations, adults in need of training and retraining, single parents and homemakers, the incarcerated, and individuals with limited English proficiency. Each of these groups are targeted as special needs populations and receive *set-aside* monies under the Carl D. Perkins Act. Within the specified 57 percent available for programs under Title II of the Act, 10 percent goes to the handicapped, 22 percent to the disadvantaged, 12 percent to adult training, 8.5 percent to single parents and homemakers, 3.5 percent to programs to eliminate sex bias, and 1 percent to the incarcerated.

Of the overall federal authorization, 50 percent of the $35 million to carry out programs related to adult training, retraining, and employment development must serve single parents and homemakers. For information on how these funds are allocated, contact your state department of vocational education. The increasing amount of federal monies and set-asides indicates the federal concern for disadvantaged students. As industrial educators we have and will continue to have a legal and social mandate to assist disadvantaged students.

The Carl D. Perkins Vocational Education Act of 1984 sets forth the following as the legal definition of disadvantaged students:

> The term *disadvantaged* means individuals (other than handi-
> capped individuals) who have economic or academic disadvan-
> tages and who require special services and assistance in order to
> enable them to succeed in vocational education programs. Such
> term includes individuals who are members of economically
> disadvantaged families, migrants, individuals who have limited
> English proficiency, and individuals who are dropouts from, or
> who are identified as potential dropouts from, secondary
> school.[1]

Economically Disadvantaged Students

It is clear from the definition above that many students can be
categorized as disadvantaged. All too often, poverty stands as the
common feature that unites disadvantaged students. According to A.
C. Lewis, in a recent article in the *Phi Delta Kappan*, the greatest
challenge facing American society—and its schools—is the increasing number of children of poverty. The article cites several studies
that document the fact that currently about 22 percent of children
under age 18 live in poverty and that disadvantaged students as a
group now represent 30 percent of the school population.[2]

Some statistics cited in the *Phi Delta Kappan* article relate specifically to the target groups identified in the Carl D. Perkins Vocational
Education Act of 1984:

● Single-parent families, those hit hardest by poverty, have
doubled since 1970 and now account for 26 percent of all families.

● Teenage pregnancy, a surefire path to poverty, has increased
dramatically in all ethnic and socioeconomic groups.

● About 700,000 students dropped out of school in 1984-85,
practically guaranteeing themselves a lifetime of unemployment or
low wages.

● The unemployment rate for those between the ages of 16 and 19
sticks at nearly 18 percent with the rate for black youths more than
double that figure.

When we consider discrimination, we normally think of factors
like race, religion, sex, or maybe age—but not economics. Yet,
economic discrimination presents a reality that can severely restrict a
student's educational opportunities. As the studies indicate, more

and more of our students stand at an economic disadvantage. Many of those who need us most, who have the most to gain from our programs, may lose the opportunity because of economic discrimination. Without purposeful intent, we may keep students like Paul from enrolling in industrial education classes.

In some cases, the fees we charge may be prohibitively expensive. Also, some students may have a false impression of project, material, or incidential expenses based on one or two other students' experiences. When assessing your policy on charging for materials or supplies, make sure to keep charges to a minimum and inform students of those charges before they enroll in a class. Also, check to see if a special fund exists at your school for students who cannot pay fees because of financial hardship. Your school may be eligible for special federal vocational funds if your community qualifies as an economically depressed area due to a high rate of unemployment or a large concentration of low-income families. Determine your school policy regarding charging for materials and familiarize yourself with your state statutes.

Because public education is not specifically identified in the United States Constitution, it falls under the jurisdiction of each individual state. Every state constitution has a section on legal responsibility for public education that provides the basis for legal interpretation regarding materials fees in educational programs. We will give relevant constitutional and case citations from representative states.

For example, the Missouri Constitution contains a section on public education similar to those found in most state constitutions. It reads, "A general diffusion of knowledge and intelligence being essential to the preservation of the rights and liberties of the people, the general assembly shall establish and maintain free public schools for the gratuitous instruction of all persons in this state within ages not in excess of 21 years as prescribed by law."[3]

In Missouri, legal decisions involving public education must be consistent with this section of the constitution. For example, a Missouri court held in *Concerned Parents* v. *Caruthersville School District* that this constitutional provision prohibits school districts from charging fees for courses taken for academic credit.[4]

Oregon offers an example of state legislation that relates specifically to charging for materials in public educational programs. It allows a school district to require payment of fees "in any program where the resultant product, in excess of minimum course requirements and at the pupil's option, becomes the personal property of the pupil."[5]

Many variables go into determining whether or not a public education program may charge for materials. In Missouri, the student's age and whether or not academic credit is granted constitute determining factors; in Oregon, the law considers whether or not the student takes home the product or activity. Whether a class is required or elective forms another common determining factor. In a New Mexico court case, *Norton* v. *Board of Education of School District No. 16*, the court held that reasonable fees may be charged for elective courses.[6] The court also recognized that the board of education should clearly define required and elective courses.

We have cited only a few state constitutions and court cases. Every state has its own interpretation on the legality of charging for school materials and supplies. Every industrial education teacher who charges students for materials should check his or her school district or college policy and state regulations with regard to specific classes. Are your classes elective or required? How old are your students? Do projects or the products of class activities become students' personal property?

Beyond familiarization and compliance with state laws and school district policies, some hard questions arise here:

- Are you teaching for the project or for the content?
- Do you offer students options in learning activities?
- Do you help students learn the value of material conservation and cost effectiveness?

Teaching for Content

One of the most exciting and rewarding aspects of industrial education—whether industrial arts or trade and industrial education—is that it gives students "hands-on" experience with the skills and concepts they learn. Good activities and projects allow students to learn things that cannot be learned in other ways. Problem solving, planning, building, and troubleshooting all form part of a project or activity that helps students "learn by doing." Unfortunately, this only holds true for well-designed and well-planned activities. A poorly conceived project can result in a lack of productivity, in hours of frustration and boredom for your students, and perhaps in an unnecessary and burdensome expense.

We must continue to give our students opportunity to participate in well-planned learning activities and projects. However, of equal importance, the project must not become an end in itself or a barrier to an economically disadvantaged student who cannot afford its cost.

One solution involves creating a better balance of projects and activities. Rather than build a course around one or two large projects, have students take part in a series of learning activities. These will likely be less expensive, more motivating, and more closely tied to course objectives. They could involve experiments that reuse materials, group projects, or the more typical take-home project. Using less expensive activities also helps disadvantaged students feel more a part of the class and reduces the risk of embarrassment.

Offering Options

Successful industrial educators have always offered students options in learning activities. When based on sound curricular goals, a variety of learning activities can help students meet class objectives. For example, students in a welding class can learn basic skills and competencies in a variety of ways. Projects, exercises that reuse material, and repair jobs are all common examples. Another example of a successful alternative strategy involves a mass-production project in which all or part of the materials costs are recovered through project sales.

Just as a mass-production activity can help students learn about manufacturing, a service-sector project can help them understand that growing and important area. Students could form a simulated service company to repair appliances in the electrical area, perform spring tune-ups and service on lawnmowers in the power area, or restore furniture in the materials/processes area. In any of these, students gain valuable hands-on experience at minimal cost. Refer to Chapter 2 for additional information on industrial education activities that involve the general public.

Teaching Conservation and Recycling

Our "throw-away" society is slowly awakening to the value of careful conservation of materials and resources. More than any other subject area, industrial education can show students firsthand the benefits of material conservation and cost effectiveness. If projects and learning activities use recycled, donated, or otherwise cost-effective materials, our students will learn the value of conservation in an immediate way. One person's junk is another's treasure. The ability to conserve and recycle is best learned by practice and example. We have a great opportunity to help our students in this area. In addition, through these practices not only do we teach conservation, but our economically disadvantaged students have a better opportunity to participate at minimal expense.

As industrial educators, we have a legal and social obligation to reach out to economically disadvantaged students. Industrial educators must operate within the guidelines of school district policy and state regulations. Beyond that, however, we have a professional responsibility to our students and their families. We cannot discriminate on the basis of a student's economic situation. By choosing wisely from the many learning activities at our disposal and readily available resources, all our students can have hands-on experience that will reach far beyond the projects they build.

Academically Disadvantaged Students

For purposes of administering the Carl D. Perkins Vocational Education Act, the academically disadvantged student is defined in the *Federal Register* as "an individual who scores at or below the 25th percentile on a standardized achievement or aptitude test, whose secondary school grades are below 2.0 on a 4.0 scale, or [who] fails to attain minimal academic competencies."[7]

This definition does not include individuals with learning disabilities. Students with diagnosed learning disabilities are considered handicapped.

However, keep in mind that a student may be handicapped though as yet untested and, thus, undiagnosed. The definition for specific learning disabilities (see Chapter 8) is broad and a handicapping condition is often difficult to detect. As a result, it is often referred to as "what's wrong when nothing is wrong." The students themselves may not realize why they have much trouble learning. Early diagnosis is important—without it, students may grow frustrated and discouraged. Seek out and talk to your school's special education teacher or specialist to find out whether a student has been properly evaluated and whether he or she has a special learning disability as defined in P.L. 94-142.

The fact that academically disadvantaged students may have difficulty in most classes does not necessarily mean they will do poorly in industrial education classes. An industrial education class may provide the spark that ignites their enthusiasm for learning. Participation in industrial education activities may serve as a catalyst for improving the self-concept and achievement level of an academically disadvantaged student.

Suggested Strategies

Use your imagination and input from other professionals when working with an academically disadvantaged student. Talk with the student's counselor, your administrator, and other teachers who have or have had the student in class. Review the student's school records. Try to determine the reasons behind a student's poor performance. Ask about any successes others may have had with the student.

If you can determine that the problems relate to reading, test anxiety, or the home environment, you will stand in a better position to help the student. If, for example, the student has difficulty with reading, use care to assign reading material at an appropriate level. Arrange for the student to work on group activities. Carefully go over and explain your instructions in a matter-of-fact manner to avoid calling extra attention to the problem. You do not have the time, materials, or expertise to teach every student to read—but you can select materials with an appropriate reading level. Recognizing the problem and showing sensitivity to the student's feelings will—with a little creativity—go a long way toward providing a successful learning experience for the academically disadvantged.

Other suggested strategies for the academically disadvantaged involve

● using task analysis to arrange material in a meaningful sequence.

● allowing students to serve as peer tutors in subjects they know well—which helps both the academically disadvantaged student and the tutor.

● familiarizing yourself with teaching methods designed for academically disadvantaged students.

● showing a patient, but not patronizing, attitude and maintaining appropriate expectations for classroom performance.

Limited English Proficiency

The third and fastest-growing category of disadvantaged students are those with limited English proficiency. The *Federal Register* defines limited English proficiency as referring to individuals:

> (1) who were not born in the United States or whose native language is a language other than English; who came from environments where a language other than English is dominant; or who are American Indian and Alaskan native students and who come from environments where a language other than English has had a significant impact on their level of English language; and
>
> (2) who by reason thereof, have sufficient difficulty speaking, reading, writing, or understanding the English language to deny those individuals the opportunity to learn successfully in classrooms where the language of instruction is English or to participate fully in our society.[8]

Students identified as being limited English proficient (LEP) by the above definition are enrolling in industrial education in record numbers. Those whose native language is Spanish, Vietnamese, or another see industrial education as a means to a good job, a higher standard of living, and a good start in a new country.

Suggested Strategies

Industrial educators can use the following methods to help limited-English-proficient students succeed. They are adapted from an article by Curtis Bradley and Joan Friedenberg.[9]

1. Convey a positive attitude. Use body language, a pleasant speaking style, and an attitude that demonstrates sensitivity for different cultures.

2. Communicate in carefully and well-thought-out English. Avoid slang or obscure references.

3. Teach job-survival skills. Many LEP students haven't learned important career education basics.

4. Modify your teaching techniques. Be flexible and sensitive to the needs of different students. Minimize lecture time and increase the time you spend on demonstrations.

5. Communicate and work with your school's English-as-a-second-language (ESL) specialist. The ESL teacher can provide information about a student's English ability as tested on a standardized instrument such as the Bilingual Oral Proficiency Test. You can work with the ESL teacher to coordinate your instruction with the student's other class instruction.

6. Use bilingual safety signs and labels.

7. Use peer tutors or bilingual teacher's aides to work with your LEP students.

These suggested strategies have been used with success by industrial education teachers involved in studies done by Bradley and Friedenberg in south Florida. Limited-English-proficient students are typically highly motivated and eager for an opportunity to participate in industrial education programs. They represent an important new group of students for industrial educators.

References and Case Citations

[1]Carl D. Perkins Vocational Education Act of 1984, Section 2.20 U.S.C., Section 2301, Section 400.4, 1984.

[2]Lewis, A. C. "Washington Report: Young and Poor in America." *Phi Delta Kappan* 67 (1985), no. 3, 251-52.

[3]Missouri Constitution of 1985, Article XI, Sections 1 and 3.

[4]Concerned Parents v. Caruthersville School District No. 18, 548 S.W. 2d 554 Mo. (1977).

[5]Oregon Revised Statute, 339.155 (5).

[6]Norton v. Board of Education of School District No. 16, 89 N.M. 470, 553 P. 2d 1277 (1976).

[7]U.S. Department of Education. "Final Regulations for the Carl D.

Perkins Act of 1984." *Federal Register* 50 (August 1985), no. 159, 33226-306.

[8]Ibid., 33234.

[9]Bradley, C. H., and J.E. Friedenberg. "Instructional Strategies for English-Speaking Trade and Industrial Education Instructors of Limited-English-Proficient Students." *Journal of Industrial Teacher Education* 22 (1985), no. 2, 52-58.

Resources

American Council of Industrial Arts Teacher Education. *Industrial Arts for Disadvantaged Youth.* Bloomington, Ill.: McKnight & McKnight, 1970.

American Vocational Association. *Vocational Education for Special Groups.* Washington, D.C.: American Vocational Association, 1976.

Cobb, R.C., and D.E. Kingsbury. "The Special Needs Provisions of the Perkins Act." *VocEd: Journal of the American Vocational Association* 60 (1985), no. 4, 33-34.

Kimeldorf, M.R. *Special Needs in Technology Education.* Worcester, Mass.: Davis Publications, 1984.

Phelps, L.A. "Issues and Options for Special Populations." *VocEd: Journal of the American Vocational Association* 59 (1984), no. 1, 33-35.

CHAPTER 8
Handicapped Students

Jerry, who has been diagnosed as mentally retarded, is main-streamed into the woodworking class along with 23 other ninth-grade students. He shares a bench with Susan, a talented student who helps and supports Jerry's efforts. Using hand tools, and with Susan's help, Jerry has made a breadboard for his mother and a toy paddlewheel boat for his little brother. Then, just as things are going well, an administrator informs the woodworking teacher that Jerry's parents have requested that he have access to the power machinery that his classmates use. Jerry's parents want him to be able to support himself someday, and breadboards and paddlewheels made with hand tools will not give him skills for future employment. The teacher can understand their reasoning and shares their concern for Jerry's future.

What steps can an educator take to help handicapped students? How does the law protect their rights in schools today? Are the rights of handicapped students on a collision course with the school's duty to provide for the health and safety of all students? How would spending an inordinate amount of time with one handicapped student affect the rights of other students in the class? This chapter will focus on these and other questions related to the rights and needs of handicapped students.

Public Law 94-142

In the fall of 1975, Congress passed legislation requiring that all handicapped children receive free and appropriate public education. Here, "free" means without charge to parents, "appropriate" calls for the provision of all services required to meet a child's educational needs, and "public" refers to education available equally to all citizens through provisions granted by federal, state, or local governments. Since its passage, the Education for All Handicapped Children Act has touched all aspects of American education. The federal regulations for Public Law 94-142 specifically include industrial education in this passage:

> Each public agency shall take steps to insure that its handicapped children have available to them the variety of educational programs and services available to nonhandicapped children in the area served by the agency including . . . industrial arts . . . and vocational education.[1]

The emergence of P.L. 94-142 and a rising number of handicapped students in industrial education classes make it increasingly important for industrial educators to know the legal rights of handicapped students. In this chapter, we will summarize pertinent sections of P.L. 94-142 and their implications for industrial educators.

Child Find

Child find attempts to ensure the location, identification, and evaluation of all handicapped children who need special education or services. It requires educators to determine which children currently receive special education and related services and which do not.

Before P.L. 94-142, a teacher might commonly have said, "Jane is not doing well in her studies because she is lazy." Today, labeling a student "lazy" does not give sufficient explanation of his or her inability to learn. We must now ask whether Jane is handicapped. If, based on your observations of classroom performance, you suspect one of your students may have a handicapping condition, you must, by law, communicate this to your school's special education teacher or director. The special education staff holds responsibility for evaluation and identification of the specific handicapping condition.

Legal Definitions of Handicapping Conditions

Every state has established procedures for identifying and evaluating handicapped students as a part of an annual program plan. At a minimum, the guidelines include the definitions of handicapping conditions found in the federal law in 45 *Federal Register* 121a.5. Here, the term *handicapped* applies to those children evaluated, in accordance with sections 121a.530-534, as mentally retarded, hard of hearing, deaf, speech impaired, visually handicapped, seriously emotionally disturbed, orthopedically impaired, other health impaired, deaf-blind, multihandicapped, or as having special learning disabilities that require special education and related services. Although the special education staff will make the final identification of a student's handicap, industrial educators should familiarize themselves with the legal definitions of handicapping conditions. This can help you identify handicapped students in your classes and better meet their needs. The following definitions of handicapping conditions, based on P.L. 94-142, are accompanied by instructional strategies you can use in industrial education classes.

Hearing Impairment

Deaf refers to a hearing problem so severe that a child is impaired in processing linguistic information through hearing, with or without amplification, which adversely affects education. *Hard of hearing* refers to hearing impairment, whether permanent or fluctuating, which adversely affects a child's educational performance but which is not included under the definition of *deaf.*

1. Install a light on dangerous machinery to indicate when the machine is on.

2. A hearing-impaired student who uses a hearing aid may be harmed by loud machinery. Consult a hearing clinician for specific recommendations.

3. Face the student and speak clearly when giving instructions. Where possible, use clearly written instructional materials that reduce the need for oral instructions. If the student has difficulty in reading, provide step-by-step illustrated instructions.

4. Use a buddy system or peer tutor to help the hearing-impaired student in both the lab and classroom.

5. Involve the hearing-impaired student in class discussion. Do not assume that a handicap limits or precludes participation in class activities.

Visual Impairment

Visually handicapped describes a visual impairment which, even with correction, adversely affects a child's educational performance. The term includes both partially sighted and blind children.

1. Take extra safety precautions here. For example, thoroughly practice what to do in case of a fire or emergency. With some practice, the visually impaired student can become acclimated to the shop and be able to reach safety without running into obstacles.

2. Provide additional orientation to equipment. With proper supervision, turn the power off and allow the student to feel and explore the different parts of a machine and how they work. Use the same process with hand tools.

3. Use three-dimensional models instead of two-dimensional plans or working drawings. Through tactile exploration, visually impaired students can comprehend the shape and size of the object without relying on drawings.

4. Use more oral instructions and tests.

5. Highlight important parts of machines, such as switches and controls, with a contrasting color.

Speech Impairment

Speech impaired refers to a communication disorder, such as stuttering, impaired articulation, language impairment, or voice impairment, that adversely affects a child's performance in an educational setting.

1. Give the speech-impaired student enough time to speak.

2. Provide phonetic spelling and correct pronunciation of new technical terms.

3. Listen for the content of what is said, not the trouble the student has in saying it.

4. Some days will be easier for this student than others. Encourage speaking in class and extra interaction with other students on good days.

5. Give the student classroom or lab responsibilities.

6. Do not allow other students to make fun of stuttering or other speech impairments.

Orthopedic Impairment

Orthopedically impaired refers to skeletal deformities that adversely affect a child's educational performance. The term includes impairments caused by congenital anomaly (e.g., clubfoot, absence of some other member), impairments caused by disease (e.g., poliomyelitis, bone tuberculosis), and impairments from other causes (e.g., cerebral palsy, amputations, and fractures or burns that cause contractures).

1. Keep aisles between equipment and machines free and clear. Remember that wheelchairs require at least five feet of clearance.

2. You may need to modify a workbench height for a student in a wheelchair. As one option, you can make a semicircular cutout in the table so the student can wheel right into it. If you can't make cutouts, consider the use of lapboards that rest on the student's wheelchair.

3. Provide extra practice or simulation in learning a psychomotor skill for students who have motor/coordination problems.

4. Consider modifications in tools and equipment. You can extend controls on machinery to permit access. Substitute foot controls for hand controls. Enlarge tool handles with padding. An occupational therapist or your special education teacher can provide more specific suggestions for tool and machinery modification.

5. Emphasize safety practices and the use of safety equipment.

Mental Retardation

Mental retardation refers to significantly subaverage general intellectual functioning, that exists concurrently with deficits in adaptive behavior, appears during the developmental period, and adversely affects a child's educational performance.

1. Involve as many senses as possible in the learning process. For example, the student might smell different woods while blindfolded or listen to the taped sound of machines.

2. Whenever possible, teach by demonstration. Don't hesitate to use hand-over-hand assistance in demonstrating tool or machine use.

3. Allow time for practice of machine or tool processes. Break complex operations into smaller, more easily accomplished tasks.

4. Provide plenty of positive reinforcement and encouragement.

Learning Disability

Specific learning disability refers to a disorder in one or more of the basic psychological processes involved in understanding or in using language, spoken or written, that may manifest itself in an imperfect ability to listen, think, read, write, spell, or do mathematical calculations. The term includes such conditions as perceptual handicaps, brain injury, minimal brain dysfunction, dyslexia, and developmental aphasia. It does not appy to children who have learning problems that primarily result from visual, hearing, or motor handicaps; mental retardation; emotional disturbance; or environmental, cultural, or economic disadvantage.

1. The learning-disabled (LD) label does not excuse the student from learning. Keep appropriate expectations for performance and remember that learning-disabled students usually have average or above average intelligence.

2. Unlike mentally retarded students, LD students are capable of abstract and complex concepts. Do not let a deficit in one area of psychological processing limit their learning.

3. Use a wide variety of approaches and instructional techniques when working with learning-disabled students. Some LD students find helpful the use of puzzles or problem-solving activities in learning new concepts.

Emotional Impairment

Serious emotional impairment refers to a condition exhibiting one or more of the following characteristics over a long period of time and to a marked degree: an inability to learn that cannot be explained by intellectual, sensory, or health factors; an inability to build or maintain satisfactory interpersonal relationships with peers and teachers; inappropriate behavior or feelings; a general, pervasive mood of unhappiness or depression; or a tendency to develop physical symptoms or fears associated with personal or school problems. The term includes children who are schizophrenic or autistic. It does not include those who are socially maladjusted, unless it is determined that they are seriously emotionally disturbed.

1. Try to build the emotionally disturbed student's self-confidence through successful activities and projects. Go easy on bad days and

avoid direct confrontations that would exacerbate the condition.

2. Provide immediate feedback and reinforcement. When emotionally disturbed students return from an absence, help them get back on track with their work. Don't allow them to remove themselves from class activity.

3. Make sure the emotionally impaired student knows fully the proper use of tools or machines.

Combinations of Handicapping Conditions

Deaf-blind refers to concomitant hearing and visual impairments, the combination of which causes such severe communication and other developmental and educational problems that the affected student cannot be accommodated in a special education program designed solely for either deaf or blind children. *Multihandicapped* means concomitant impairments (such as *mentally retarded-blind* or *mentally retarded-orthopedically impaired*), the combination of which causes such severe educational problems that the affected student cannot be accommodated in special education programs designed solely for one of the impairments. This term does not apply to deaf-blind children.

When working with a student who has a combination of handicapping conditions, use some of the strategies identified for each of the individual conditions.

Other Health Impairment

Other health impaired students have limited strength, vitality, or alertness due to chronic or acute health problems such as heart condition, tuberculosis, rheumatic fever, nephritis, asthma, sickle-cell anemia, hemophilia, epilepsy, lead poisoning, leukemia, or diabetes.

1. Check regularly with your school nurse to learn whether any of your students has a health condition that may have side effects or require special medication. For example, if you have a student who suffers from epilepsy, you would want to know the severity of the attacks and what to do if an attack occurs.

2. A student with asthma may need to use a special respirator or mask while working in woodshop or metal shop.

As you can see, there are many different handicapping conditions that can affect the performance of your industrial education students. While you will not make the final diagnosis of a handicapping condition, as an instructor you stand in the best position to identify potential problems a handicapped student may encounter in an industrial education class and to design effective teaching strategies.

Individualized Education Plan

Every child identified as handicapped must have a written individualized education plan (IEP) developed jointly by the child's parents or guardian and at least two representatives from the school. One must be qualified to provide or supervise special education and the other must be someone who will have instructional contact with the child. If appropriate, the child may attend the meetings. P.L. 94-142 states that every IEP must contain at least statements of

1. the student's present levels of educational performance based on evaluation in all relevant skill areas;

2. annual goals, including short-term instructional objectives;

3. specific educational services to be provided;

4. the extent to which the child can participate in regular education programs;

5. the projected date for instruction and anticipated duration of the educational programs;

6. appropriate objective criteria, evaluation procedures, and schedules for determining on at least an annual basis whether the student is achieving instructional objectives.

Begin working with a handicapped student who may be placed in an industrial education class *before* the decision is made. Let your administrator or special education teacher know that you would like to participate in an IEP meeting for a student who may enroll in your class. Before the meeting, observe the handicapped student in another class setting to identify questions regarding the student's condition and educational placement. As a participant in the IEP meeting, you can then provide valuable information and answer questions regarding the student's placement. Information you might bring to an IEP meeting includes (1) an overview of the industrial education program and individual classes; (2) potential health and safety problems; and (3) an assessment of educational goals that are realistic or compatible with the existing industrial education program.

At the meeting, you might ask questions concerning the student's (1) previous work experience related to industrial education, (2) career goals, (3) interests and hobbies, (4) specific impairments that may significantly impact performance in your class, and (5) skills the student will need before entering your class.

You can recommend that a handicapped student who has never taken a shop or lab course first receive special instruction to prepare for an industrial education class. The special education teacher can help you prepare the student. You can also help identify special services and resources the student will need during your course to meet educational objectives.

Related Services

Public Law 94-142 defines an appropriate education in terms of specially designed instruction that meets the unique needs of the child, as specified by the IEP. Related services are those required services that can help a handicapped student fully benefit from the educational program. The regulations identify 13 related services: audiology, counseling services, early identification, medical services, occupational therapy, parent counseling and training, physical therapy, psychological services, school health services, in-school social work services, speech pathology, transporation, and recreation.

No one student may need all these services, but if a needed service is not made available, denial of access to an appropriate program will likely exist. Schools cannot deny services simply because they do not have them. They must obtain them for a student when deemed appropriate through the IEP.

For example, the United States Supreme Court, in *Irving Independent School District* v. *Tatro*[2] in 1984, held that clear intermittent catheterization (CIC) is a related service under P.L. 94-142. Born with spina bifida, eight-year-old Amber Tatro could not empty her bladder normally. She required catheterization, which involves inserting a steel tube into the bladder to remove urine. School officials argued the service would unduly burden the district and would expose it to possible lawsuits if catheterization was performed incorrectly. The Supreme Court unanimously agreed that without catheterization, Amber could not attend school and thereby benefit from special education. The court reasoned that "[s]ervices like CIC that permit a child to remain at school during the day are no less related to the effort to educate than are services that enable the child to reach, enter, or exit the school."[3] Citing cost and competence factors, the Court concluded that CIC is a simple procedure that can be provided by a school nurse and does not fit under the Act's medical exclusion.

In addition to necessary related services, schools must provide access to all educational programs and activities in public schools. Section 504 of the Rehabilitation Act of 1973, P.L. 93-516, established requirements for nondiscrimination on the basis of handicap in preschool, elementary, secondary, and adult education programs and activities. Specifically the Act states that:

● new facilities must be constructed to be accessible and usable from a program standpoint by all handicapped students.

● although the total school need not be totally physically accessible, there must be an assurance that programs conducted in those facilities are made accessible.

● structural changes should be made expeditiously to make programs accessible.[4]

Federal legislation also provides funding for related services and physical modifications needed to meet the educational needs of handicapped students. The Vocational Education Act of 1963 and its amendments in 1968 and 1984 provide specific funding for the delivery of vocational education to the handicapped. For information on assistance, contact your state department of vocational education. By participating in IEP meetings and helping set educational objectives for handicapped students, you can identify necessary related services, resources, and funding.

Least-Restrictive Alternative

Before P.L. 94-142, most handicapped children were isolated from the other students and assigned to a special room for the entire school day. Parents often complained that such separation harmed their child's social and academic development. Many parents requested that their handicapped children participate in a regular classroom setting. P.L. 94-142 addresses those concerns.

Handicapped children are now assured by law that, to the maximum extent appropriate, they will receive education with non-handicapped children. Special classes, separate schooling, or removal of handicapped children from the regular educational environment should only occur when the nature and severity of the handicap precludes satisfactory achievement of education in regular classes with the use of supplementary aid and services.

Providing the *least-restrictive alternative* for handicapped students is often referred to as "mainstreaming." As a direct result of P.L. 94-142 and the increased attention to handicapped students, more and more handicapped students find themselves mainstreamed into industrial education classes. The critical decision of whether a handicapped student should enter in an industrial education class occurs in the IEP meeting. We cannot overemphasize the importance of participating in any IEP meeting involving a handicapped student who may be placed in an industrial education class.

The decision to mainstream handicapped students into an industrial education class will be based on the educational opportunities available to that student. You cannot deny a handicapped student access to your program because you lack the appropriate facilities or equipment, curricular materials, or expertise. However, you stand in the best position to establish whether the handicapped student can meet his or her educational objectives by participating in your class.

Only a few cases involving handicapped students have been argued before the United States Supreme Court. One gives educators direction on how far public schools must go in providing related services to a mainstreamed student. A 1982 decision in *Hendrick Hudson District Board of Education* v. *Rowley*[5] interpreted "free appropriate public education" under P.L. 94-142 to generally favor, and defer to, local and state education agencies.

Amy Rowley, a deaf student, was mainstreamed into a regular first-grade classroom. Amy's individualized educational program required that she receive special services from an instructor for the deaf one hour each day and from a speech therapist three hours each week. Amy could read lips and was progressing along with the class at approximtely a "B" grade level. Her parents argued that P.L. 94-142 entitled her to the services of a qualified sign-language interpreter in all academic classes. They presented evidence that Amy was very bright and had the ability to be an "A" student. They, therefore, wanted all the support services necessary for her to achieve her full potential. The lower court agreed with her parents' argument and held she should receive "an opportunity to achieve her full potential commensurate with the opportunity provided to nonhandicapped children."[6]

The Supreme Court rejected this commensurate opportunity standard along with alternative interpretations requiring maximum opportunity or self-sufficiency. Rather, the Court held that the free appropriate public education requirement is met "by providing personalized instruction with sufficient support services to permit the child to benefit educationally from that instruction." The Court also detailed this reviewing standard for courts considering P.L. 94-142 cases: "First, has the State complied with the procedures set forth in the act? And second, is the [resulting IEP] reasonably calculated to enable the child to receive educational benefits?"[7]

The Court's dissenting opinion criticized the minimal nature of the majority's standard, suggesting that it could be met merely by giving a deaf student "a teacher with a loud voice, for she would benefit from that service."[8]

Taken together, the *Rowley* and *Tatro* cases appear to give educators mixed signals. *Rowley*, with its educational benefit test, provides us with a minimalistic, pro-school-district interpretation of the "appropriate education" requirement in P.L. 94-142. On the other hand, *Tatro* appears prostudent and expansionist in nature, implying that unless a handicapped student receives all necessary related services, the student will not benefit educationally from instruction. In other words, *Tatro* seems to require maximum effort on the part of the school to provide the related services the handicapped student will need to acheive the minimal educational benefit required by the Rowley ruling.

What does all this mean to an industrial educator who has a handicapped student mainstreamed into his or her class? Simply stated, public education must make every effort to provide the related services and structural changes necessary to accommodate handicapped students in regular classes. In an industrial education class, necessary structural changes may include modifying machines, removing barriers, or building ramps and platforms. Related services may include providing a peer tutor, supplemental instruction, or specially designed learning activities.

On the other hand, the measured educational benefit to the mainstreamed student need only be minimal and does not require maximum opportunity or self-sufficiency as long as the handicapped student is working toward the goals identified in his or her IEP. For example, the parents in the situation described at the beginning of this chapter, who wanted their son to use power machinery, may not legally be able to force their desires on the school. The professional judgment of the industrial education teacher may hold that the student is making progress, perhaps only minimal, but commensurate with his abilities.

Procedural Safeguards

Before passage of P.L. 94-142, lawyers could not participate in the school's procedure to determine the best educational programs for handicapped students. The law considered this an educational decision best decided only by parents and educators. It viewed lawyers, and the "due process" they represent, as unnecessary and not related to the educational decision. Now, however, P.L. 94-142 provides due process rights to parents in the identification, evaluation, and educational placement of handicapped children. This due process begins when the school first initiates evaluation and testing of a student suspected of being handicapped, and it continues throughout the IEP process. If parents do not agree with the IEP developed by the school district, they may request a hearing to determine an appropriate education for their child. P.L. 94-142 identifies these minimum due-process requirements:

1. A written notification before evaluation. In addition, parents have a right to an interpreter/translator if their primary language is not English.

2. A written notification before a change in educational placement.

3. A periodic review of the student's educational placement.

4. An opportunity for an impartial hearing including the right to (a) receive timely and specific notice of such hearings, (b) review all records, (c) obtain an independent evaluation, (d) have representation by counsel (a lawyer if desired), (e) cross-examine witnesses, (f) present witnesses on the child's behalf, (g) present evidence, (h) receive a complete and accurate record of the proceedings, and (i) appeal the decision of the hearings officer.

5. An assignment of a surrogate parent or guardian when the child's parents or guardian is not known, the child's parents are unavailable, or the child is a ward of the state.

6. Access to all educational records.

Due-process hearings are costly and very time consuming. Therefore, most school districts make every effort to compromise with parents. If an industrial educator is involved in a hearing, it would be as an expert testifying in the field of his or her expertise or as the student's teacher. Be prepared to testify, and recognize that you are the person best able to provide a professional opinion.

For good reason, more and more handicapped students are participating in industrial education classes. Industrial education classes offer a valuable addition to a handicapped student's educational programs. They can help handicapped students prepare for a future job, develop consumer skills related to tools and technology, and improve their self-image. We have a legal responsibility to provide educational opportunities for all students in the least restrictive environment. Aside from that obligation, handicapped students present an opportunity for industrial educators to work with new resources in developing new programs of instruction.

Recommendations

You can reach out to a new group of students and improve your effectiveness in working with handicapped students by considering the following five recommendations:

1. Partcipate actively in the IEP meetings for any student who may be placed in your classes. Help make decisions related to placement in an industrial education class, required related services, development of educational goals and objectives, and evaluation methods.

2. Communicate with the special education staff. Inform them when you need assistance or additional resources to work with a handicapped student. Let them know if you suspect that student has a handicapping condition that impairs educational performance.

3. Review and revise your curriculum for each handicapped student. Modify your class to help a student achieve the objectives outlined in his or her IEP.

4. Use alternative instructional strategies. Design projects and activities that will make it easier for a handicapped student to

accomplish your objective. Use peer tutors to help handicapped students—it will prove a worthwhile activity for both students.

5. Identify additional resources and funds to assist your work. The federal vocational acts set aside funds for handicapped students. Work with your administration to secure the resources and funding you need to help your handicapped students.

References and Case Citations

[1]Education for All Handicapped Children Act. Section 102(a), 305.

[2]Irving Independent School District v. Tatro, 468 U.S. (1984).

[3]Ibid.

[4]Rehabilitation Act of 1973, P.L. 93-516, Section 504 Regulations, Subpart C.

[5]Hendrick Hudson v. Rowley, 458 U.S. 176 (1982).

[6]Ibid.

[7]Ibid.

[8]Ibid.

Resources

American Industrial Arts Association Special Needs Committee. "Practical Answers to Common Questions about Special Needs Students." *The Technology Teacher* 44 (1985), no. 4, 10-11.

Barbacovi, D. R., and R. W. Clelland. *Public Law 94-142: Special Education in Transition.* Washington, D.C.: American Association of School Administrators, 1978.

Cremins, J. J. *Legal and Political Issues in Special Education.* St. Louis, Mo.: C. C. Thomas, 1983.

Data Research Inc. *Handicapped Students and Special Education.* Rosemount, Minn.: Data Research Inc., 1985.

Gill, Douglas. *Working with Special Needs Students: A Handbook for Vocational Education Teachers.* Atlanta, Ga.: Georgia Department of Education, 1982.

Goldberg, Stephen S. *Special Education Law: A Guide for Parents, Advocates, and Educators.* New York: Plenum Publishers, 1982.

Kimeldorf, Martin R. *Special Needs in Technology Education.* Worcester, Mass.: Davis Publications, 1984.

Martin, Reed. *Educating Handicapped Children: The Legal Mandate.* Champaign, Ill.: Research Press, 1979.

National School Boards Association. *Preventing and Defending Suits by Handicapped Students.* Washington, D.C.: National School Boards Association, 1982.

National School Boards Association. *Schools and the Law of the Handicapped.* Washington, D.C.: National School Boards Association, 1983.

Scott, John L., and Michelle D. Sarkees. *Vocational Special Needs: Preparing T & I Teachers.* Alsip, Ill.: American Technical Publishers, 1982.

Thomas, S. B. *Legal Issues in Special Education.* Topeka, Kan.: National Organization on Legal Problems of Education, 1985.

Tindall, Lloyd. *Puzzled about Educating Special Needs Students?* Madison, Wisc.: Wisconsin Vocational Studies Center, 1980.

Turnbull, H. R., and A. Turnbull. *Free Appropriate Public Education: Law and Implementation.* Denver, Colo.: Love Publishing, 1982.

Turner, S. B. *Legal Issues in Education of the Handicapped.* Bloomington, Ind.: Phi Delta Kappa, 1983.

Vocational Education Special Needs Project. *Students With Special Needs: Who Are They?* Corvallis, Oreg.: Vocational Education Department, Oregon State University, 1984.

CHAPTER 9

School Rules
and Student Searches

The high school drafting teacher is starting her first year of teaching. On the first day of classes, the teaching schedule is clear, she has a preliminary class list, and she has put some of last year's better drawings on the board. The school buses arrive, and the teacher hears the students noisily trying out their new lockers.

The first students enter the class. The teacher looks up to see a boy wearing a sweatshirt with what the teacher considers a pervasively vulgar statement printed on it. Another boy, wearing a large coat, appears to have just taken a compass from the top of a drawing board and slipped it into his pocket. As the girl next to him turns around in her seat, bubble gum explodes across her face. On the other side of the room, two boys push and yell at each other. Taking all this in, the teacher realizes she's going to have to establish some rules and procedures to help her and her students get on with the business of learning, as well as to maintain and protect school property.

What kind of academic and behavioral rules are teachers allowed to use in their classrooms? Do we have to put all rules in writing and give each student a copy, or can we just announce them? How does the U.S. Constitution affect the rules we use? Can rules in industrial education classes differ from rules in other classes? If you find tools or materials missing, can you search your students? These are some of the issues we'll discuss in this chapter as we look at school rules and student searches.

Creating Class Rules

You do not create classroom rules in a vacuum. Your rules must reinforce and carry out the guidelines set by your school board. You cannot legally enforce any rule that violates your school or school district policies or guidelines.

Before establishing rules for your program, carefully review school district and school building rules. You may find copies of the rules in your school library. They will certainly be available at the district office. Make sure you read both your building rules for teachers and your school's student handbook to obtain a complete picture of the rules that you and your students already have an obligation to follow. You must heed all established rules whether or not you agree with them. If you want to change a rule, appeal it through your administration and possibly to the school board. Failing to follow already established rules is usually considered insubordination.

All students need consistency in discipline and can usually immediately spot inconsistency or hypocrisy in the content or application of rules. Rather than ignore discrepancies in rules that could hurt your program, recognize and do something about them. If you can present well-reasoned evidence for an exception or variance to a school rule in your situation, your classroom may be legally considered "differently situated."

For example, a school rule states that students may not wear hats in school. However, you have several metals-class students, both boys and girls, who have long hair. While they operate rotating machinery, such as the lathe or drill press, their hair might get caught in the equipment. Consequently, you may have set as a class rule: "While operating rotating machinery, students with long hair must restrain their hair or wear a hat." Although your rule does not agree with the school rule, it may for safety reasons constitute a reasonable exception because your students are differently situated.

Legal History of School Rules

Until the early 1970s, court decisions tended to support the concept of *in loco parentis*, which means the school legally stands in place of a parent. Because children have no constitutional rights in their home, this meant that students in public schools had no constitutional rights. Children are protected from their parents not by the Constitution but by state and federal legislation such as child-abuse and child-labor laws. For all practical purposes, the school held complete responsibility over students in its charge, provided that school rules were made in good faith, were reasonable, and did not exceed the school's legal authority.

In the past, unless a school rule appeared clearly abusive, courts did not become involved. They left decisions on school rules to educators and local school boards. Any school rule was assumed legal, making a student responsible to prove to the court that a rule was unreasonable, capricious, arbitrary, or promulgated in bad faith. Because students and their parents could rarely overcome this burden of proof, yesterday's school rules were seldom litigated. The courts overturned them only when they were clearly abusive to students.

Constitutional Rights of Students

Today, however, the courts interpret students' rights differently. Although several cases preceded *Tinker* v. *Des Moines Independent School District*, legal scholars view this 1969 U.S. Supreme Court case as the beginning of students' constitutional rights in the public schools.[1] The case involved several students suspended for wearing black armbands in protest of U.S. military participation in Viet Nam. Here, the court stated: "First Amendment rights, applied in light of the special characteristics of the school environment, are available to teachers and students. It can hardly be argued that either students or teachers shed their constitutional rights to freedom of speech or expression at the schoolhouse gate."

Subsequent cases expanded students' First Amendment rights to include not only speech, but press and, of course, religious issues. The Fourteenth Amendment due process and equal protection clauses and the Fourth Amendment reasonable search and seizure rights also formed the basis of many court decisions on school rules.

It's a big step from the days when school rules were presumed legal and the student carried the burden of proof, to the present, where the school must protect the student's constitutional rights. However, allowing students their constitutional rights does not necessarily mean the school must give up control over students' behavior. Today, our schools hold a responsibility to balance individual rights guaranteed to students by the Constitution with society's legitimate interest in providing an effective and efficient public school system.

Compelling State Interest

A school or teacher today must have a compelling state interest to promulgate a rule that takes away a student's constitutional right. *Compelling state interest* simply means that the needs of society or the state are greater than the individual constitutional rights of the students in your class.

What does all this mean to today's industrial education teacher? When students ask why they must wear a cap when using the lathe, you should *not* tell them—as you may have in the past—"Because I said so!" You *should* say instead, "Let me tell you the compelling state interest for your wearing a hat." You then explain the state's compelling interest in the safety of its students. There may not appear much difference in the two approaches, but legally your choice can determine whether the court sustains your rule or finds you in violation of students' constitutional rights because of arbitrary and unreasonable conduct.

While you may not need to change any class rules now in common use, you may need to consider changing your approach to what rules you make and how you implement and enforce them. By devoting attention to balancing each student's individual rights with the rights of the rest of the class, you teach respect for the individual and, at the same time, help students learn their responsibility to the entire group. In other words, students today walk into your classroom with their constitutional rights and you can only deny those rights if you can show a compelling state interest.

How can you determine whether it's in the state's best interest to have a rule that may deny students' constitutional rights? The courts recognize four basic compelling state interests that outweigh students' individual rights:

- legitimate educational purpose,
- risk of property loss or damage,
- threat to health or safety, and
- serious disruption of the educational process.

If any of these four serve as the basis for your rule, it should stand the test in today's courtroom and should also make sense to a protesting student. Not only do these compelling state interests take precedence over individual student rights, but your responsibility and duty as an officer of the state *requires* that you carry out the state's interests in maintaining a safe, disciplined, and educational environment. In certain situations, you not only have the legal right to deny a student's constitutional right but must, as a requirement of your job, do so.

When evaluating the rules most industrial educators use in light of the state's compelling interest, you'll find that most fall under one of the four categories listed above. However, a rule that stands outside these categories may be "a rule for a rule's sake" or one based on personal bias. This sort of rule is not of interest to the state and may infact infringe on your students' civil rights. Let's take a closer look at how these four compelling state interests affect typical industrial education rules.

Legitimate Educational Purpose

Examples: "All homework assignments must be completed and handed in by the specified date." "At the end of each period, all tools and equipment must be properly cared for and put away." "The compulsory school laws state that you must be in school."

As the teacher, you hold responsibility for carrying out a program of instruction in your subject area. The courts will not rely on their legal background to overturn an academic decision based on sound professional judgment in educational and curricular matters. Plagiarism, classroom and homework assignments, proper tool storage, workplace maintenance, systems of grading, and any other classroom procedures designed for the educational benefit of students offer examples that fall under this category. Therefore, all rules that have a planned educational purpose tied to your class objectives would meet this standard. They should have little difficulty meeting a challenge in court.

Property Loss or Damage

Examples: "Do not use chisels as screwdrivers." "Do not damage or steal other students' property." "Do not place gum under the seats or desks."

Industrial education classes differ from others in many ways. Students in industrial education use a wide variety of state-owned tools and equipment to complete learning activities. They work on activities over time ranging anywhere from a single class period to an entire year. The industrial education teacher acts as custodian of state property and has responsibility for its proper care and maintenance. Students have no viable legal argument in saying that their parents' taxes support the schools and that they therefore have the right to use tools contrary to your reasonable rules. The compelling state interest in reasonable regulations to protect the state's property weighs greater than the students' right to use equipment when, where, and as they choose. If your rules for protecting state property are fair and educationally sound, you will have no problem in the courts.

Threat to Health or Safety

Examples: "Students must wear safety glasses while using rotating machinery." "Students are not allowed to use a machine until they pass a safety test." "Always use the exhaust hose when a car is running."

The industrial education teacher has a very important responsibility to provide for the health and safety of students and others who may be in the shop area or who may use products produced by his or her program. While students may complain about wearing safety glasses or hardhats, passing tests, seeing the school nurse, or wearing a hairnet, you stand on solid legal ground when you prevent those who refuse to follow the rules from using the school's tools and equipment—or, for that matter, from being in the shop at all. Industrial education classes provide many students' first opportunity to learn safe and responsible use of tools and equipment. A strong, consistently enforced health-and-safety policy helps students develop habits that will benefit them the rest of their lives. Society places a high priority on the health and safety of its citizenry and will go to great lengths to support rules designed for their protection. Your rules should be well thought out, very visible, and strictly enforced.

Serious Disruption of the Educational Process

Examples: "No horseplay in class." "Do not use power machinery during instruction." "Do not bother other students working on individual projects."

Industrial education classes differ from most others in that they offer a wide variety of student activities that can occur at varied times and, many times, in different locations. As in a physical education class, students may in a typical period move throughout the lab performing a variety of activities, some in groups and others as individuals. High levels of noise from machines, tools, and the students themselves may be quite normal. You must be able to distinguish between acceptable behavior and unacceptable behavior that seriously disrupts the educational process. Regardless of the activity—demonstration, individual project, or class lecture—the state clearly has an interest in keeping a classroom free from disruptive behavior that detracts from other students' learning and the teacher's efforts to teach.

Developing Rules

Keep rules simple and straightforward and as limited in number as will get the job done. Excessive rules are confusing to students, hard to remember, difficult to enforce, and usually distract from learning. The following four steps provide guidelines for developing and implementing fair and reasonable rules: (1) Determine the rules most important to your teaching situation. (2) Write and state them as clearly and concisely as possible. (3) Give every student a copy of your rules at the beginning of the term or year. (4) Review and discuss them carefully with each class, explaining the basis or reason for each rule. Note any absent students and make sure they receive the same rules and explanations you gave their classmates.

Providing notice of rules forms a fundamental step in meeting the requirements of the due process clause of the Fourteenth Amendment. Failing to give students proper notice is tantamount legally to having no rules at all. Again, consider what you want to accomplish, write your rules carefully, make sure every student gets a copy, and take time to explain and answer questions. Not only will this help prevent injuries and create a good learning environment, but it will also help your attorney defend you in the event of a legal cause of action arising from class activities.

The basic rules for your class should be written broadly and followed by, but not limited to, specific examples usually based on your past experiences. These examples flesh out and enhance the meaning of your broad general rules. They provide the needed notice to students regarding what you mean by a rule that reads, for example, "Do not damage the tools and equipment." Unless you use specific examples of how tools are damaged, you have not given adequate notice to students. Legally, this is commonly called the "vice of vagueness."

You can use the four compelling state interests presented earlier as your broad general rules and follow with specific examples under each category. The courts do not limit you to the rules you established at the beginning of the class but allow additions and deletions as accidents or events that you did not foresee occur during the school year. In almost every case, your new rules would address a specific situation that falls under one of the broadly written basic rules already formulated. As new situations arise and you promulgate relevant rules during the school year, discuss the additions with your class and make sure each student—again, including those absent—receives a written copy.

Every teacher today faces the challenge of balancing the state's interest in maintaining a good learning environment with students' individual rights. Teachers usually find it more difficult to enforce ironclad rules based on personal bias or "rules for rules' sake" than to promulgate rules that allow students their rights and use compelling state interests to take away those rights. If your rules show respect for students' individual rights, if you make students responsible for their academic efforts and manner of dealing with others, and if you are firm and fair in applying your rules, you will have fewer injuries, better discipline, and a likelihood of maintaining an effective learning environment for students.

Student Searches

The Fourth Amendment of the United States Constitution forbids "unreasonable searches and seizures" by government officials and provides that warrants "describing the place to be searched and the persons or things to be seized" can be issued only "upon probable cause." The amendment applies in school situations when a state or federal criminal prosecution develops based on evidence obtained on school premises with the involvement of school authorities. In addition, the Fourth Amendment is sometimes mentioned in connection with the concept of the right of "an expectancy of privacy"—a right also associated with the concept of liberty derived from the Four-teenth Amendment.

Periodically, industrial education teachers have reason to search students who they suspect of hiding such things as tools, materials, drugs, or even something they may have taken from another student in class. In most instances, the teacher only wants to get the school property back, get the drugs out of circulation, or return a stolen item to its owner. In the past, teachers have waded right in, demanding that pockets be emptied, coats opened, or lockers cleared out, in order to locate missing items. This somewhat oppressive and heavy-handed approach has given way today because of students' rights under the Fourth Amendment, which require teachers and adminis-trators to search for and seize suspected contraband and prohibited items in students' possession in a fair and reasonable manner.

New Jersey v. T.L.O.

Reasonable procedure has been interpreted for public school edu-cators in the 1985 United States Supreme Court case of *New Jersey* v. *T.L.O.*[2] There have been many lower court decision on the question of student searches, but until *T.L.O.* the United States Supreme Court had remained silent on the issue. Because the Court's jurisdic-tion affects all lower courts throughout the United States, *T.L.O.* has become the decision on which we must base our classroom proce-dures. To really profit from the court's decision and to be able to apply it correctly in everyday situations, we must fully understand the facts of the situation and the court's decision in this landmark case of student Fourth Amendment rights in the public schools.

The case involved a 14-year-old girl, T.L.O., whom a teacher observed smoking in a girl's restroom in violation of school rules. The teacher took the girl to an assistant principal's office. T.L.O. denied smoking in the restroom and claimed that she did not smoke at all. At this point, the assistant principal took T.L.O. to a private office where he asked to examine the contents of her purse. He wanted to see whether she had any cigarettes, believing the presence of cigarettes would support the accusation that T.L.O. had been smoking. T.L.O. complied and the assistant principal observed in her purse a package of cigarettes. As he removed the cigarettes, he found a package of rolling papers and removed them, too. Based on his experience that rolling papers signalled the possibility of marijuana use, he looked further in the purse and found the following items: (1) a metal pipe used to smoke loose marijuana, (2) a plastic bag containing marijuana, (3) $40 in one-dollar bills and $.98 in change, (4) an index card titled "people who owe me money," followed by a list of names and amounts of $1 or $1.50 by each name, (5) two letters, one from T.L.O. to a friend and a response from the friend, both referring to the sale of marijuana at school.

The assistant principal called T.L.O.'s mother and the police. T.L.O. subsequently admitted to the police her involvement in selling marijuana to other students and was charged with possession of marijuana with the intent to distribute. In criminal court, T.L.O. moved to have the evidence taken from her purse by the assistant principal excluded from her trial on the grounds that the search violated her rights under the Fourth Amendment. Her motion was denied and she was found guilty of delinquency and placed on one year's probation.

Justice White's majority opinion upholding the trial court's decision answers three questions that are important to industrial educators: (1) Do students have constitutional rights in school? White answered yes. (2) Do students have Fourth Amendment rights in school? White said yes. (3) Are school officials state actors in public schools (i.e., does state action exist)? Again, White answered yes.

Justice White analyzed what is reasonable under the Fourth Amendment in a public school situation and found that such a determination requires balancing "the individual's legitimate expectations of privacy and personal security" against "the government's need for effective methods to deal with breaches of public order." The majority of the court determined that the warrant requirement was "unsuited to the school environment" and held "that student officials need not obtain a warrant before searching a student who is under their authority." The court went on to state that in its place "the legality of a search of a student should depend simply on the reasonableness, under all the circumstances, of the search." Reasonableness involves a two-fold inquiry: First, one must consider whether an action was justified at its inception. Second, one must determine whether the search as conducted was reasonably related in scope to the circumstances that justified the interference in the first place.

White then had to decide whether the law he announced, if applied to the facts, made the search of T.L.O. reasonable. He began his conclusion by dividing the search into two searches—one for cigarettes and one for marijuana. The court found the search for the cigarettes reasonable, arguing that possession of cigarettes would both corroborate the report that T.L.O. had been smoking and undermine the credibility of her defense to the charge. The search, therefore, met the reasonable-suspicion test. Continuing the same logical reasoning, the Court determined that the assistant principal's second search, once he saw the rolling paper, was also reasonable and, again, met the second test of being reasonably related in scope to the circumstances of the initial search.

Implications for Industrial Educators

A big question faces industrial educators who must make decisions on a daily basis that apply these legal standards: Just what evidence is relevant and necessary to determining reasonableness? White's opinion helps to provide an answer. He writes that evidence "need not conclusively prove the ultimate fact in issue, but only have any tendency to make the existence of any fact that is of consequence to the determination of the action more probable or less probable than it would be without the evidence." In other words, the teacher must have at least some shred of evidence or reason to suspect a student is hiding or has possession of something in violation of school policy. A teacher's decision to go through all students' lockers "just to see what might turn up" would of course lack reasonable cause and thus would violate students' Fourth Amendment rights. However, if a student reports seeing a package of what looks like heroin in another student's locker, this would provide the reasonable suspicion necessary for a teacher to legally search the locker in question, regardless of whether heroin is in fact in the locker.

Random searches of student lockers occasionally are found to be legal if the teacher can show a compelling state interest for conducting a search. For example, at the end of each semester many schools try to locate lost or stolen tools and materials by searching all students' lockers. This type of search clearly falls under the state's interest in maintaining its property. It is very important, however, that the teacher advise students of this practice and warn them in advance of coming locker searches, explaining the reasons behind the search. This adds to the teacher's integrity in the eyes of the students and lets them know the teacher will not sneak around behind their backs. Whenever possible, have a student present when conducting a search of his or her locker. If the student is absent during a search, you risk the possibility of being accused of taking something for your own use from the locker or simply of invading the student's privacy. When the student cannot be present, ask another adult to witness your search and record what you take from the locker. Although students may lose some of their rights of privacy, they do not give up their right to notice. Failing to provide some form of notice may result in an illegal search. If a tool is missing at the end of class, a *random* search of all the lockers or students before they leave the classroom would be an infringement on their constitutional rights. On other hand, if you had reasonable suspicion that a specific student was concealing one of the shop's tools, searching that student would certainly be considered reasonable.

Another example that falls under health-and-safety concerns involves a search of all student lockers after a school receives a bomb threat. In a clear emergency, we can all expect to lose our constitutional rights rather quickly. In this type of situation, notice to the students is not necessary because of the life-threatening nature of the problem. Except for emergencies and periodic searches for school property, however, random searches of students or their lockers for exploratory reasons is not advised.

Another practice sometimes abused in educational settings involves taking student property and either failing ever to return it or keeping it until the end of the school year. This happens in most cases with such items as squirt guns, knives, or new "fads" that come along, which when used during class usually disrupt the educational process. Although school rules may prohibit students having an item, the teacher here is still converting the student's property to his or her own use. Conversion, under the law, is defined as any distinct act of dominion wrongfully exerted over another's personal property in denial of or inconsistent with his or her rights, such as a tortious taking of another's chattels.

You may choose an innovative or creative way to return students' property, but make sure you do return it within a reasonable period of time. If the situation involves an illegal possession of drugs, firearms, or contraband of some kind, turn the item or substance over to your adminstrator or law enforcement authorities. Ask for a receipt to protect yourself from the embarrassment of having the student or others accuse you of keeping and using the property for yourself. You might also consider giving receipts to students whose property you take. This practice implies professionalism and a serious regard for the incident in question.

The ruling in the T.L.O. case also speaks to the issue of a student's expectancy of privacy. The court record does not detail the method the assistant principal used to get T.L.O.'s purse away from her, but in a situation where a student refuses to hand over a purse or empty his or her pockets, the teacher might encounter problems even if he or she has a reasonable suspicion of a violation of a rule. To wrestle a student to the floor just to search the student's pockets may result in injury to someone and may even be judged illegal. When a student refuses a reasonable request and you feel something has to be done, contact your administrator, who in some situations may decide to call in law-enforcement officers to conduct the search. In the event of dangerous weapons or explosives, where imminent danger to students and faculty exists, the law allows reasonable necessary physical force. Use your best judgment here—the standard you will be judged by in the end will be whether you used *reasonable* physical force. You must still think of your job as primarily that of "educator." Your job description is not likely to include the responsibility of physically forcing a reasonable search.

The courts are much more stringent in applying protections to a search of a student's person than to a search of his or her locker. This seems only natural since a personal search involves much greater interference with privacy, and the Fourth Amendment basically intends to address protection of an individual's privacy. This has brought about another issue schools must face in student search litigation: the demand for money damages for violation of constitutional rights. Consider the situation in one of the first cases on the subject, *Picha* v. *Wielgos*, an Illinois case that involved the strip search of three female students.[3] Unlike most school search cases in which the student is the defendant in a criminal prosecution or similar juvenile proceeding, in *Picha* v. *Wielgos* the students acted as plaintiffs, suing school administrators for damages under Section 1983 of Title 42. This civil rights act often forms the basis of civil suits arising from student suspensions and free speech issues. While the court's ruling was complicated by the involvement of police in the search, and while no actual damages were awarded, the court found that school administrators could be held liable for such damages. This suggests that particular caution must now be exercised, especially in personal searches of this kind.

The courts agree that strip searches of students are illegal in the absence of search warrants or probable cause. Although the volatile issue of strip searches was not decided in *T.L.O.*, it is likely the Supreme Court would agree with lower court decisions that have litigated the matter. The majority opinion's second prong of the reasonableness test for a school search—whether the "measures adopted are intrusive in light of the age and sex of the student and the nature of the infraction"—can be interpreted as an implicit warning for school officials to use good judgment and refrain from strip searches of students.

Although *T.L.O.* has provided some guidelines for school teachers and administrators, we cannot view it as answering all the questions that will arise in school search situations. The Supreme Court's 1985 decision has only affirmed the consistent holding of lower federal courts that school officials may base a search of a student on a reasonable belief that the student has violated a school rule or poses a threat to the school environment and that warrants and probable cause are not required in school searches. The Court has reserved for future review issues of police involvement in school searches, individualized suspicion, and expectation of privacy involving inanimate objects. It did not have before it the facts on which to consider issues of dog sniffing that leads to school searches, strip searches, liability for illegal searches, and the use of illegally obtained evidence at school disciplinary proceedings. Answers to these unresolved questions must be found in the lower federal courts and in the respective state courts that have litigated the problems.

Educators will find that the courts differ widely from one jurisdiction to another. Yet by staying abreast of regional case law, reading professional journals, and regularly attending conferences and seminars for educators, industrial education teachers and administrators should be able to keep up with new decisions that may change school policy and procedures in the future. This can be an emotionally charged and volatile area of the law for teachers and administrators. Careful steps, therefore, should always be taken to insure respect of the Fourth Amendment and to give encouragement and support for the industrial educator's informed and responsible behavior.

Citations

[1]Tinker v. Des Moines Independent School District, 89 S.Ct.733 (1969).

[2]New Jersey v. T.L.O., 105 S.Ct.733 (1985).

[3]Picha v. Wielgos, 410 F. Supp. 1214, N.D. Ill. (1967).

Resources

Elam, Stanley M. *Public Schools and the First Amendment: Conference Proceedings.* Bloomington, Ind.: Phi Delta Kappa, 1983.

Strope, John L. *School Activities and the Law.* Reston, Va.: The National Association of Secondary School Principals, 1984.

Lemerer, Frank R., and Kenneth L. Deutsch. *Constitutional Rights and Student Life: Value Conflict in Law and Education.* St. Paul, Minn.: West Publishing Co., 1979.

Reutter, Edmund E., Jr. *The Supreme Court's Impact on Public Education.* Bloomington, Ind., and Topeka, Kan.: Phi Delta Kappa and National Organization on Legal Problems of Education, 1982.

Millington, William G. *The Law and the College Student.* St. Paul, Minn.: West Publishing Co., 1979.

CHAPTER 10
Due Process
and the Rights of Teachers

The deteriorating condition of the metal shop has frustrated and concerned the vocational teacher for several years. The shop area's small size, the lack of space between machines, the age of the equipment, and the inadequate ventilation system have inspired numerous memos to the principal over the last year and a half. As a last resort to get some action and prevent serious injuries to students, the teacher decides to describe these problems in the letters-to-the-editor section of the local newspaper. The first response to his letter comes the next day in the form of a message from the principal asking to see him as soon as possible. Before he can close the door behind himself, the principal starts with very pointed remarks about the inappropriateness and inaccuracy of his very conspicuous letter. She does all the talking, giving the teacher no time to comment or explain, and finishes by telling him that she will immediately initiate a dismissal proceeding against him on the grounds of insubordination. As the teacher leaves her office, he is thankful that he has tenure. Then he begins to wonder whether tenure addresses professional differences of opinion and the right to express an opinion in public.

What are the rights of teachers in a dismissal process and when do they begin? Are these rights different for tenured and nontenured teachers, and for public and private teachers? Does a teacher's First Amendment right of free speech allow him or her to express an opinion on school issues? What other constitutional protections do public school teachers have? Situations such as the one described above are usually very disquieting and in some instances are traumatic enough to ruin a teaching career. Today, teachers find it increasingly important to familiarize themselves with their constitutional rights and with state and local laws on education. Industrial educators who know their legal rights and responsibilities will find themselves better prepared to make day-by-day decisions and will demonstrate greater buoyancy and resilience if adversity strikes. With this in mind, we will examine the teacher's due process rights of the Fourteenth Amendment along with other constitutional and statutory rights affecting public school teachers today.

Defining Due Process

The rights protecting teachers all have their origin in the United States Constitution, and the *due process* we discuss has its genesis in the Fourteenth Amendment to that constitution. The Fourteenth Amendment reads in part ". . . nor shall any State deprive any person of life, liberty, or property, without due process of law."

Although very short and precise, the Due Process Clause has gone through nearly 200 years and thousands of court decisions that clarify and interpret its meaning. Picture blind justice with her arms outstretched holding her scale. On one side of the scale visualize a heap of bodies and on the other, one lone industrial education teacher. Due process in its simplest terms constitutes the law's effort to balance the individual rights of a single person with the necessity of protecting society as a whole. To understand the enormous depth of this constitutional concept and to appreciate its complexity, let's examine this clause a few words at a time.

"[N]or shall any State" means that in order to have a right to due process, state action must occur. For example, when applied to education, only teachers in public schools have Fourteenth Amendment rights; teachers in private schools do not. The legal rights of faculty in private schools are expressly set in the contract of employment between the school and its teachers. A teacher dismissed from a private school has only those rights specified in the contract. If a teacher feels dissatisfied with the rules of a private school, the courts advise the teacher to negotiate contract changes or find a job in a school with acceptable rules. On the other hand, in public schools that force students to attend through compulsory state attendance laws and that reimburse faculty with state funding, state action exists. Along with the taxpayers' money, comes the teacher's due process rights of the Fourteenth Amendment and government patterns of increased job security.

"[D]eprive any person" refers to withholding constitutional rights from any person within the jurisdiction of the United States. It applies to both citizens and noncitizens—even to those noncitizens present in the United States illegally. This does not imply that illegal aliens have a right to live here, but they do have the right to due process while here, as well as to the legal proceedings which may lead to their deportation. It also applies to "persons" created by law such as corporations and partnerships. "Any person" is broadly interpreted by the courts and now includes students in public schools.

"[O]f life, liberty, or property" refers to those rights of which a person may not be deprived. Note that the framers of our Constitution used just three words to protect our past, present, and future, and address even our death at the hands of the government. The word "property" includes everything a person owns and has acquired to the present. It covers such tangible properties as real estate, personal property, and money, and such intangibles as contracts of employment and eligibility and entitlement to welfare payments. It encompasses all tangibles and intangibles that we own and have a right to keep and possess. The word "liberty" begins with the present and embodies all future acquisitions and aspirations.

> [I]t denotes not merely freedom from bodily restraint but also the right of the individual to contract, to engage in any of the common occupations of life, to acquire useful knowledge, to marry, establish a home and bring up children, to worship God according to the dictates of his own conscience, and generally to enjoy those privileges long recognized. . . as essential to the orderly pursuit of happiness by free men.[1]

The word "life" refers to the loss of life at the hands of the government—in other words, the execution of a criminal. Stated in positive terms, a state may deprive a person of life, liberty, or property only if the individual receives due process.

"[W]ithout due process of law" refers to the *process due* persons by the local, state, and federal government. Court decisions have separated due process into two distinct aspects—substantive and procedural—to facilitate its application to everyday situations. It is important here to delineate the two aspects in order to understand the application of due process to public education.

Substantive due process pertains to legislation, or the rule or law itself. To deprive a person of life, liberty, or property, the state must have a valid objective and the means used must be reasonably calculated to achieve the objective. A rule must:

1. have some rational need for adoption,

2. be approximately as good in meeting the need of the state as any alternative that reasonable people would have developed, and

3. be supported by relevant and substantial evidence and findings of fact.

In other words, substantive due process requires that the rules or laws in question be minimally rational and reasonable before the state can deprive someone of life, liberty, or property. Whenever someone questions a rule or seeks clarification of a decision, he or she legally exercises Fourteenth Amendment substantive due process rights.

Procedural due process relates to the decision-making process followed in determining whether a rule or law has been violated. Basic fairness in adjudication is required and has been interpreted by the courts as including (1) adequate notice, (2) a fair and impartial hearing, and (3) the right to appeal the decision.

Adequate notice covers such points as the charges of the law violated, the evidence to be used against the person charged, the availability of a reasonable amount of time to prepare a defense, notification of the time and place of a hearing, and adequacy of form (whether oral or written). A fair and impartial hearing encompasses elements such as a meaningful opportunity to be heard, opportunity to state a position, opportunity to present witnesses, the right to counsel, an opportunity to present and cross-examine witnesses, and access to written reports in advance of a hearing. The right of appeal not only applies to our state and federal court system but has an integral part in our governmental structure as well. A public school administrator who tells you he or she has made an unappealable decision is probably wrong. With few exceptions, the due process clause allows for appeal of all administrative interpretations and decisions, as well as the law or rule in question, all the way up to the school board through the district's administrative structure. From the school board, the decision or rule is appealable to either a higher state or federal administrative agency, and from there to an appropriate court. Alternatively, it is appealable directly from the school board to a state or federal trial court. Once in the court system, any rule or decision in question may someday appear on the docket of the United States Supreme Court. Every rule or decision made in public schools is subject to review by another person, board, or court. Most students and teachers do not realize that they have the right to appeal any educational decision or policy, and that their appeal may go all the way to the United States Supreme Court.

As with many legal concepts, due process resists definition in the dictionary sense and tends to be a dynamic, rather than static, concept. With this thought in mind, and serving as a qualifier for the remainder of this chapter, we hope to breathe life into and extract some meaning from the so-called "rights" we so often hear about. As a next step, we will assimilate these legal concepts into day-by-day professional activities and responsibilities. Let us begin with the procedural and substantive due process rights of teacher contracts and dismissal procedures.

Nontenured Teachers

In recent years, many industrial education teachers have found employment as nontenured teachers. It is not uncommon for community college technical education programs to have significantly more part-time nontenured teachers than full-time tenured teachers. It is therefore important to know that there are two basic types of contracts for nontenured teachers. The first, called a fixed-term or temporary contract, is characterized by definite beginning and ending dates of intended employment. Enforceability of a temporary contract will depend on whether the teacher fully understood that employment would not extend beyond the closing date agreed to in the contract. The quality of the teacher's performance during that period and the availability of continued funding for the position has no relevance. In other words, a public school teacher's Fourteenth Amendment right of "notice" regarding termination is met when he or she agrees to a dismissal date before employment begins. A breach during the term of the contract, however, would result in full due process rights.

The second type of nontenured contract, a continuing contract, is usually issued to teachers annually in the spring or summer for the school year beginning the following fall. Teachers signing these yearly contracts are called "probationary" in most states and have an expectancy of contract renewal each year. The expectancy of contract renewal can be legally revoked, however, if the employer meets the teacher's Fourteenth Amendment procedural due process rights to notice, a fair hearing, and an appeal. The procedural rights appear in state laws and are quite explicit as to the process that must be followed. They normally include a written statement of the reasons for dismissal or nonrenewal; a date, usually in the spring, by which the teacher must receive notice of nonrenewal; the right to representation and a fair hearing; and the right to appeal the school board's decision.

Although it first appears the probationary teacher has considerable due process rights, most states limit appeal of the board's decision only to procedural questions of notice and fair hearing. They do not allow the courts to consider the board's reasons for dismissal or nonrenewal, unless those reasons violate the teacher's constitutional rights or the school board acted in bad faith. Probationary teachers have, by law, only procedural due process rights and essentially have no substantive due process rights. As long as the school board acts in good faith and gives adequate notice and a fair hearing, appeal is limited to the procedures used in the dismissal or nonrenewal. Beginning industrial education teachers should review their state law because the situation differs from state to state.

Tenured Teachers

The educational tenure system is controversial and frequently misunderstood. The general public often wonders why public school teachers should have the protection of a tenure system when most other employees do not. In fact, a public school teacher at a social gathering with a group of noneducators might very likely hear someone say, "If we could get rid of the tenure system in our public schools, we could fire our poor teachers and hire good ones who would improve education." A teacher knowledgeable about tenure and teachers' constitutional rights might respond by saying, "There are two good things about the tenure system." This conversation stopper may draw the attention of everyone in the room, and someone will invariably say, "Well, if you're so smart, name *one* good thing about it." Now on the spot, and perhaps feeling defensive, our teacher might begin by saying, "First of all, tenure protects a 'good' teacher from unfair dismissal."

Tenure laws give competent teachers assurance of continued employment as long as they perform satisfactorily. With tenure protection, a teacher can be dismissed only for cause and only in accordance with procedures specified by law. Tenure laws attempt to meet procedural due process outlined earlier in the discussion on nontenured teachers as well as the other aspect, substantive due process. Unlike the nontenured teacher, the tenured teacher's appeal of a hearing rests not only on the school board's good faith and the fairness of the process itself but on specific statutory reasons the school board must allege and prove true. It is not uncommon to hear of a teacher being fired because of a personality conflict with an administrator, a professional difference of opinion, or seemingly for no reason at all. It is in the public's interest that its employees have protection from arbitrary and capricious decisions. Tenure first benefits public education in that it allows "good" teachers to teach without suffering the anxieties and apprehensions associated with supervision by an incompetent and ineffectual administrator or a vindictive and malicious school board.

Although acquiring tenured status gives a teacher a vested interest in continued employment, it does not guarantee permanent employment. Dismissal of a tenured teacher must be based on causes identified in state laws. As state laws grant provision for tenure, they also grant provision under which tenure can be revoked. Causes included in these laws vary considerably among the states, from an extensive listing of individual grounds to a simple statement that dismissal must be based on cause. The usual grounds for dismissal are incompetency, immorality, and insubordination.

Incompetency has been construed by the courts to mean any physical or mental condition that tends to incapacitate a teacher's effective performance. This rather broad definition generally concerns a fitness to teach, which contains a wide range of factors. It has been used by many boards as a catchall for teacher dismissal. Immorality is subject to wide interpretation and includes such issues as criminal activity, sexually related conduct between a teacher and student, and sexual orientation and lifestyle issues like those involving a pregnant single teacher or an unmarried teacher who lives with a member of the opposite sex. Insubordination, on the other hand, is narrower and imports willful disregard for an employer's express or implied directions and repeated refusal to obey reasonable regulations. The tenured teacher's protection against dismissal involves his or her substantive due process rights. To take a teacher's job, the school board must have reasons it can substantiate.

Most of the people involved in the hypothetical conversation begun earlier in this chapter probably have known a teacher or had a personal experience with a poor administrator and may agree that society should have laws that protect good teachers. While accepting that there's one good thing about tenure, someone in the group may be unable to imagine a second benefit and may come back with a surly, "And what's the second thing that's so good about tenure?" "Tenure provides an orderly procedure for dealing with a 'poor' teacher," our teacher responds. The spirited general reaction to this second point goes something like, "Then why doesn't this orderly procedure get rid of so and so down at the school who everybody in town knows is a poor teacher." It surprises most people that the orderly procedure allowed a poor teacher is nothing more than the procedural and substantive due process rights of the Fourteenth Amendment. Many years of court decisions and administrative hearings have clarified the orderly procedure that an administration must provide a poor teacher in a fair dismissal.

The process due teachers in a dismissal starts with the teacher's constitutional right to adequate notice. Before being dismissed from any job, an employee must know what his or her job entails. Usually written in very broad terms, a teacher's job description typically includes such items as teaching assignments, coaching responsibilities, and other general language concerning what a teacher of a particular subject or grade level should be able to teach or do. In short, the typical teacher's job description is very vague and would hardly meet the constitutional standard of adequate notice under procedural due process rights. An administrator must clarify in greater detail what the teacher's job requires and must inform the teacher how well expected performance standards are met.

Most state laws require periodic evaluations and conferences to apprise teachers of the quality of their teaching performance and to elaborate details of the job not covered in the general job description. Through this process, the job description becomes more specific through discussion and documentation of management problems and teaching inadequacies. The discussions notify the teacher that something is wrong and provide an opportunity for the teacher and administrator to generate ideas to deal with identified problems. In most states, routine evaluations and conferences involve all the faculty, not only those teachers experiencing problems. However, if problems persist without improvement after the required evaluations and conferences, a good administrator will move to the next phase, becoming more specific about the teacher's job description. The administrator will also consider further ideas and activities to help the teacher improve teaching performance.

Some states refer to this next step as a "plan of assistance for improvement." The plan essentially requires written notification that the teacher's performance has fallen below acceptable standards; that the teacher needs assistance; and that the principal and teacher will confer, study the deficient performance, and plan a corrective program. The plan defines the performance to be improved, a schedule for making improvement, and provision for monitoring progress. Generally, a timetable, usually lasting three to five months, is agreed on. It allows the teacher a reasonable time to remedy deficient performance. During this time, the school district must provide assistance to help the teacher achieve stated performance goals. Assistance by the school district might include release time to observe other teachers or help from specialists within and outside the district—for example, industrial training, counseling and therapeutic services, or funding for workshops and college courses the administrator feels will further the teacher's professional development.

At this point in providing the teacher adequate due process, the administrator must do everything reasonably possible to help the teacher achieve performance goals. Without making a sincere and good-faith effort to help the teacher improve, the administrator has no reason to continue the fair dismissal process. If the administrator had already decided to dismiss the teacher at the time of instituting the plan of assistance for improvement, most courts would rule against dismissal due to inadequate notice and lack of a good-faith effort to help the teacher improve. Adequate notice requires that everything the administrator has done to this point be designed and implemented solely to help the teacher succeed. Because of the employer-employee association, a duty has been created by law and with it responsibility on the employer's part to help the employee learn the job and become effective and productive. An employer cannot hire someone for a job, then immediately begin a process to dismiss that employee. Formation of a relationship of trust requires that the employer do everything possible to insure the success of the employee.

If the teacher does not succeed after a reasonable period of time that includes a good-faith effort on the part of the administration, the next step in the dismissal process acknowledges a departure from the trust relationship. This stage is called an adversarial relationship. The teacher receives written notification of a change of status, which, while clearly not a notice of dismissal, nevertheless, advises the teacher that from the present date to completion of employment, or until another conclusion is reached, the supervision and consultation used under the plan of assistance for improvement will no longer go solely toward the improvement of deficiencies. It will also be used to obtain and record information that may determine the teacher's continued employment by the school district. In this way, the teacher receives adequate notice of the discontinuance of the trust relationship and of a possible dismissal hearing. At a dismissal hearing, evidence introduced to show cause could be based on the observations and evaluations documented from the date of the change of status. The administrator and teacher now stand legally at arm's length until dismissal or another conclusion is reached.

The remaining procedures for dismissal are well established in state laws and should be followed precisely. Dismissal of a poor teacher is usually very stressful and time consuming. If carried out with full understanding and appreciation of the teacher's constitutional rights, however, the teacher will, in part, feel grateful to the administrator for the time and effort expended and will leave with respect for the professional conduct shown in handling a difficult situation.

In 1985, the United States Supreme Court, in *Cleveland Board of Education* v. *Loudermill*, decided a landmark case that mandates a new procedure in public employee dismissal cases.[2] The facts in the case reveal that Loudermill was hired as a security guard by the Cleveland Board of Education. A question on his job application asked whether he had ever been convicted of a felony. He answered no. His employer subsequently discovered that Loudermill had been convicted of grand larceny and dismissed him for his dishonesty in not disclosing his felony conviction. Loudermill argued that he did not report the conviction because he believed it was a misdemeanor, not a felony, and that if granted a pretermination hearing, he could have explained the circumstances surrounding his alleged dishonesty. The Supreme Court agreed with Loudermill.

The court held that the pretermination hearing (1) need not be elaborate—it can be "something less" than a full evidentiary hearing; (2) need not definitely resolve the propriety of the discharge but must produce enough information to constitute an initial check against a mistaken decision; (3) should determine the existence of reasonable grounds for believing that the charges against the employee are true and support the action; and (4) should offer an opportunity to respond and present reasons, in person or in writing, as to why the proposed action should not be taken.

This case appears to add another step to the dismissal process of a public school teacher by holding that a minimum procedural hearing must occur in every dismissal if the employee has a job right. Apparently, all public employers today face two hearings before they can legally dismiss an employee. The ramifications of this case are sure to have a broad and far-reaching effect on the rights of public school teachers and to add another responsibility to the legal duties of public school administrators.

Freedom of Expression

Public school teachers' status regarding their rights of free expression has received considerable court attention over the last two decades. Historically, public employees have enjoyed a limited right of public expression, with speaking out on issues considered a privilege rather than a right. The traditional judicial view joined the notion that the reward for government employees' increased job security allowed the forfeiture of certain constitutional rights, such as the right to express one's belief about the government. However, starting in the 1960s, an increased concern with individual rights, combined with a seemingly receptive federal judiciary, resulted in some teachers challenging the legal weight of authority that teachers had traded their rights for increased job security. Several Supreme Court cases and numerous lower court decisions give public school teachers today general guidelines on just how far they can go with certain behavior and what speech is protected by the United States Constitution.

The 1968 Supreme Court decision of *Pickering* v. *Board of Education* established for the first time the First Amendment right of freedom of expresion for public school teachers.[3] In this case, Pickering was dismissed from his position for writing a letter published in a newspaper that criticized the school board's actions. These actions included certain allocations of school funds between educational and athletic programs and the board's and superintendent's methods of informing, or neglecting to inform, the school district's taxpayers of the real reasons the district sought additional tax revenues. The board, labelling that letter detrimental to the best interests of the schools, dismissed Pickering from his teaching position for insubordination. The Court held for Pickering, noting that the public has crucial interest in having free and unhindered debate on matters of public importance and that teachers are, as a class, the community members most likely to have informed and definite opinions about the spending of funds allotted to school operation. Thus, the Court held it essential that public school teachers be able to speak freely on such issues.

In balancing the teacher's interest in expressing views on public issues and the board's interest in efficiently operating the school district, the Supreme Court advanced two tests: (1) Did the question presented involve maintaining either discipline by immediate superiors or harmony among co-workers? (2) Did the statements impede the teacher's classroom performance or the normal operation of the school? Although the Court allows teachers to speak out on issues of broad public concern, it gives them no constitutional right to speak on topics that would jeopardize their ability to perform as a teacher. Teachers should keep these kinds of concerns internal and proceed through the grievance process provided by the collective-bargaining agreement or by school board policy.

This *balancing-of-interests* test has dominated subsequent cases that further define a teacher's right to freedom of speech and expression. The Eighth Circuit Court of Appeals upheld the dismissal of a teacher who encouraged students to oppose army recruiters visiting campus during the Vietnam War.[4] The algebra teacher in question told his students they should "get [the recruiters] in a crowd, and push them and kick them, and make them feel like they weren't wanted." The court applied the Pickering criteria and found that the teacher's remarks interfered with the operation of the school, were unrelated to his class, and created a potentially disruptive situation. Speech designed to incite to action and create a disruption is not constitutionally protected, and the court upheld the teacher's dismissal.

However, if a teacher's expression does not interfere with an employer-employee relationship or threaten normal school operations, it is unlikely that it can be silenced simply because it is unpopular with school authorities. In another case, a teacher's wearing of a black armband in silent protest of the war in Vietnam was found by the Second Circuit Court of Appeals to be "speech" and not to be disruptive and, therefore, to be constitutionally protected.[5] The question is often not *what* statement is made, but *how* the statement is made. Although the administration did not agree with the teacher's statement about the Vietnam War, it could not prove the teacher's "speech" was disruptive to the educational process.

In 1983, the United States Supreme Court, in *Connick* v. *Myers*, clarified the right of a public employee to speak out on matters of private interest, not to the public this time but within the organization itself.[6] In this case, an assistant district attorney created a disruptive situation in the office by circulating a questionnaire that solicited the views of 15 other assistant district attorneys concerning office transfer policy, office morale, the need for a grievance committee, and the level of confidence in supervisors, and asked whether they felt pressured to work for political campaigns. Myers was terminated because of her refusal to accept a transfer and was told that her distribution of the questionnaire was an act of insubordination. The Supreme Court upheld her dismissal, stating that all matters that transpire within a government office are not necessarily of public concern. "While as a matter of good judgment, public officials should be receptive to constructive criticism offered by their employees, the First Amendment does not require a public office to be run as a roundtable for employee complaints over internal office affairs."

The Connick case does not mean that teachers will have no opportunity to speak out on issues or to influence the goals and management of the schools. Nor does *Connick* reverse *Pickering* and its descendants. *Connick* does, however, establish a fine, but perceptible, line between unlawful disruption in the school and lawful criticism of the principal's management of the school. "Internal assassins," though, will probably have to change their tactics. This case clearly suggests that a teacher with a complaint should go directly to an administrator and stay within the grievance process provided by the district. If not satisfied with the resolution of the grievance, the teacher should find another teaching position or be prepared to face termination.

Dress and Appearance

In the past, teachers have challenged regulations governing their dress and appearance as violating constitutionally protected rights to privacy, free expression, and personal liberty. While the Supreme Court has not directly addressed grooming standards for teachers, it has upheld the right of other public employers to impose reasonable regulations on employee appearance. A classic argument between school board and teacher appeared in the United States Second Circuit Court of Appeals through the complaint of a male teacher who had been reprimanded for not complying with that part of his school's dress code that required him to wear a tie in the classroom.[7] The teacher was cleanly attired in a jacket and sport shirt without a tie. The board gave as reasons for the regulation that it establishes a professional image for teachers, promotes good grooming among students, and encourages respect and decorum in the classroom. As reasons for not wearing a tie, the teacher stated that he wished to present himself to his students as a person not tied to "establishment conformity;" that he wished to symbolically show his association with the ideas of the students' generation, including the rejection of many of the customs and values and the social outlook of the older generation; and that he felt that tieless dress enabled him to achieve a closer rapport with his students and thus enhanced his ability to teach. The court majority rejected the idea that the teacher's action represented symbolic speech protected by the First Amendment. With respect to the assertion that concepts of academic freedom were invaded, the court made it clear that it saw no reason to give preference to the teacher's effort to indoctrinate his students with values "implicit in tielessness" over the board's desire to inculcate the values it associated with wearing ties. The Court found irrelevant the teacher's arguments regarding his constitutional rights of liberty, free speech, and academic freedom. The question was one of curriculum and who decides the social and educational values students will learn. That question has been answered many times by the court, and the school board clearly has final authority to decide curriculum matters.

An industrial educator who chooses not to wear a tie because of potential safety hazard would have a legitimate reason for his decision. But other reasonable regulations that impose no threat to safety or inteference with the teaching of industrial education are enforceable if a rational basis for the rules exist. Arbitrary regulations, however, are not enforceable and are vulnerable to challenge as a violation of personal liberty.

Salary Schedules

The law does not require that teachers new to a school system receive from a local school board credit on the salary schedule for teaching or other work experience outside the system. If the board decides to grant credit, it may do so on the basis of an examination of each case, according to fixed or negotiated rules, or by a combination of the two methods. School boards commonly give credit for work experience other than teaching that relates to or is closely connected to a teaching field. For example, industrial educators many times receive credit for work as mechanics, carpenters, machinists, or television repairmen. Military service, Peace Corps, VISTA, and other public service units represent other sources for credit given to new industrial education teachers entering the system.

Where qualifications and performance are the same, teachers must be treated the same. However, position titles alone are not controlling. For example, the Supreme Court of Minnesota sustained a decision by a local school board that teachers in a special vocational-technical school be treated differently, as a class, from teachers of vocational subjects in the regular secondary schools because their qualifications differed.[8]

Assignment and Transfer

Assigning teachers to individual school buildings lies within the discretion of the school administration and the local school board. Teachers have no legal rights to specific building assignments. However, local boards of education frequently adopt rules governing transfers and give teachers employed within the district first chance at a vacancy occurring in another school in their district. After a district adopts these rules, the courts will require it to follow its own transfer policy.

Teachers must accept reasonable teaching assignments in their areas of competence and within the scope of their teaching certificate. Some states allow misassignments or teaching outside the teacher's certified field for one to two periods a day. If a separate certificate is not required for a position, any teacher can legally be assigned to that position. This is of particular interest to industrial arts teachers who typically have certification to teach all areas of industrial arts education in grades K-12. Teaching high school woodworking for 10 years does not preclude a teacher's transfer to a general junior high program. On the other hand, a vocationally certified teacher could not be permanently assigned to a full-time industrial arts teaching schedule at a junior high. You should familiarize yourself with the language and intent of your teaching certificate.

As a general rule, teachers may be assigned to reasonable extra-duty activities, although collective-bargaining contracts vary greatly in the extent to which the teacher's duties are detailed. Collective-bargaining contracts tend to include more provisions than individual contracts, but there remains the question of a teacher's implied obligation under the contract to perform duties not enumerated in it. Unless the contract language specifies otherwise, teachers may be assigned to such activities as supervision of a study hall, conducting student-parent conferences, accompanying students on bus trips, and organizing and advising student-parent activities, as well as the always-present supervising of athletic events. Courts hold that assignments like these are all a part of the job of teaching and, thus, lie within the duties implied in the teacher's contract.

Right to Privacy

A teacher serves as a role model for students, exerting a subtle but important influence over their perceptions and values. The courts, over the years, have expected a teacher's character and conduct to be above those of the average person not working in so sensitive a relationship as that between teacher and student. Changing life-styles and frequent lack of agreement regarding "proper" conduct may make it difficult for teachers to know when they might transgress a norm or exceed school or community expectations. This problem is heightened by the fact that the definition of acceptable teacher conduct varies from one school district to another. Behavior acceptable in a metropolitan area, because of its large population and relative privacy, may not be tolerated in a small town, where everyone seems to know what everyone else does.

Since state laws cite "immorality" as a ground for teacher dismissal, courts have been called upon repeatedly to adjudicate issues dealing with controversial life-styles. These issues have included homosexuality, adultery, unmarried members of the opposite sex living together, unwed pregnant teachers, sex-change operations, and sexual advances by teachers toward students. Although court decisions have not been consistent, they have determined that in areas of personal conduct teachers do not necessarily have to be perfect. An overriding factor, and the fundamental issue in most cases, involves whether the life-style or indiscretion in question seriously affects the teacher's effectiveness as a teacher. Where a teacher's professional achievement is unaffected and the school community is placed in no jeopardy, a teacher's private acts are his or her own business and may not form a basis for discipline. Courts have demonstrated a reluctance to enforce or bar conduct solely on the basis of conformity, historical precedent, or "expert" opinion. Rather, they have required a connection between the conduct in question and actual teaching performance.

There appears no consistency in the courts' treatment of homosexual teachers, adultery, or unmarried couples living together. They have generally not upheld dismissals of teachers for being unmarried and pregnant but they have consistently upheld dismissals based on sexual advances toward students. The weight of authority, particularly more recent authority, holds that merely being arrested and charged with a criminal act does not, in and of itself, constitute a basis for dismissal. Conversely, a school board can dismiss a teacher found not guilty of charges related to ones that the board considers reasonable grounds for the teacher's dismissal. The board may conduct its own hearing independent of the criminal proceeding and base a teacher's discharge solely on its own investigation and evidence.

Leaves of Absence

Paid sick leave provides a teacher compensation due to absence because of illness or injury. State laws or district policy govern the number of days allowed each year and normally permit accumulation of an unlimited number of days. Some states permit a school employee to take a fixed number of accumulated sick-leave days to other school districts in a move from one district to another. Retiring teachers may often apply unused sick-leave days to the amount of time worked in the system, which can result in a substantial increase in income during retirement years. Paid sick leave is also available to women who are disabled due to pregnancy or childbirth.

Maternity leave is ordinarily negotiated by each teacher directly with the district personnel office and varies from a few months to a year, depending on the teacher's individual needs and desires. With the advent of Title IX of the Education Amendment of 1972 and state laws on sex discrimination, denying a teacher reasonable leave time for maternity would constitute discrimination on the basis of sex. A district cannot force a pregnant teacher to leave before the birth of her child, nor can it require that she remain away from her job for a certain period of time after the birth of a child. The pregnant teacher today has the right to decide when she will leave and return to her teaching position. Once the teacher negotiates maternity leave, however, the district can legally hold the teacher to the agreement.

Not all religious holidays or celebrations fall during school vacations and teachers who seek to worship on days during the school week must receive leave time. Title VII of the Civil Rights Act of 1964 prohibits discrimination against employees on the basis of religion. Courts interpreting this federal law hold that the employer must make every effort to accommodate the religious practices of their employees and not discriminate in assignments or expectations. For example, if a Seventh Day Adventist requests that he or she not receive supervision duty at a Friday-night game, the principal must change the supervision assignment to a game on another night. On the other hand, if the employer can show that the employee's religious practice creates an undue hardship for the employer and seriously disrupts the performance of duties, the employer can legally deny the teacher the religious leave time or assignment request. Many districts negotiate several paid personal leave days each year that teachers may choose to take for religious reasons. If personal leave days are not available, emergency leave or other leave in which the teacher would reimburse the district for the cost of a substitute teacher must be granted by the administrator to accommodate a teacher's religious rights.

Recommendations

No teacher or administrator wants to become embroiled in grievance proceedings. Such proceedings are time consuming, counterproductive, and damaging to everyone involved. It is in the best interest of everyone to work together to resolve disagreements and to provide quality educational programs. However, in those instances where an industrial education teacher or administrator must become involved in a grievance proceeding, the following five recommendations will help.

1. Keep all professional records and correspondence in a secure place. These should include such documents as teaching contracts, teaching certificates, records of workshops attended, an updated resume, transcripts, evaluations, and all written communication to and from administrators. If you are not sure whether or not to keep a document, keep it.

2. Familiarize yourself with state rules and regulations on the rights of probationary and tenured teachers. Stay abreast of recent court decisions interpreting state and local rules and regulations. Be flexible to any resulting changes you may have to make in your private or professional life.

3. If you have a grievance or concern, share it with your administrator. He or she has legal responsibility to help you succeed as a teacher and must know your problems to offer help. Deal with important matters immediately—do not allow things to get out of hand. Remember, too, to keep your opinions in house and proceed through appropriate channels with your grievances.

4. If you feel you are in trouble with your administrator or have proceedings initiated against you, seek good legal advice or assistance from your professional association representative. You may

think of yourself as well informed about your legal rights, but on the battlefield of due process and constitutional interpretations, consider yourself a new recruit and seek the best counsel available.

5. Work with your administration on a professional development plan. Know the school district's needs and how your administrator sees your future with the program. Take every opportunity to apprise district personnel of your goals and aspirations. Make them aware of your strengths and your interest in helping to build a strong, vigorous industrial education program.

Case Citations

[1]Myer v. Nebraska, 262 U.S. 390, 399 (1923).

[2]Cleveland Board of Education v. Loudermill, 105 S.Ct. 1487 (1985).

[3]Pickering v. Board of Education of Twp. High School District 205, 392 U.S. 563 (1968).

[4]Birdwell v. Hazelwood School District, 491 F. 2nd 490 (1974).

[5]James v. Board of Education of Central School District Number 1, Addison, 461 F. 2nd 566 (1972).

[6]Connick v. Myers, 461 U.S. 138 (1983).

[7]East Hartford Education Association v. Board of Education of the Town of East Hartford, 564 F. 2nd 838 (1977).

[8]Frisk v. Board of Education of Duluth, 75 N.W. 2nd 504 (1956).

Resources

Alexander, Kern, and M. David Alexander. *The Law of Schools, Students and Teachers in a Nutshell.* St. Paul, Minn.: West Publishing Co., 1984.

Cobb, Joseph J. *An Introduction to Educational Law for Administrators and Teachers.* St. Louis, Mo.: C.C. Thomas, 1981.

Hollander, Patricia. *A Legal Handbook for Educators.* Boulder, Colo.: Westview, 1978.

Lowe, David, and Annette Watters. *Legal Research for Educators.* Bloomington, Ind.: Phi Delta Kappa, 1984.

Mawdsley, R., and S. Permuth. *Legal Problems of Religious and Private Schools.* Topeka, Kan.: National Organization on Legal Problems of Education, 1983.

Munro, Robert J. *Grievance Arbitration Procedure: Legal and Policy Guidelines for Public Schools, Community Colleges and Higher Education.* Port Washington, N.Y.: Associated Faculty Press, 1982.

O'Reilly, Robert, and Edward Green. *School Law for the Practitioner.* Westport, Conn.: Greenwood Press, 1983.

Saalfield, Albrecht, and National Association of Independent Schools. *A Legal Primer for Independent Schools.* Boston, Mass.: NAIS, 1983.

Yudof, Mark G., David L. Kirp, Tyll Geel, and Betsy Levin. *Educational Policy and the Law.* Second ed. Berkeley, Calif.: McCutchan Publishing, 1982.

Editors of Legal Notes for Education. *1980-81 Deskbook Encyclopedia of American School Law.* Rosemount, Minn.: Informational Research Systems, 1981.

CHAPTER 11
Ethics

An important and intimate relationship exists between law and ethics. In our pursuit of common goals, we establish laws, guidelines, and policies to help resolve conflict and accomplish objectives. In addition to laws, policies, and guidelines, we each respond to social, personal, and professional ethics. In the first 10 chapters of this book, we have presented and discussed legal considerations related to critical issues that confront industrial educators. However, not all critical issues that industrial educators face are covered by law. As industrial educators make important decisions each day, they are influenced—in addition to the law—by the ethical and moral considerations that arise in each given situation.

Although there is a close relationship between law and ethics, the two are different. An industrial educator's action might be legal but unethical or ethical but illegal. *Webster's Dictionary* defines *ethical* as "conforming to accepted professional standards of conduct" and *ethics* as "the principles of conduct governing an individual or a group."[1] Warren Gauerke in his book *Legal and Ethical Responsibilities of School Personnel* commented, "What is generally called the ethics of a profession is actually but consensus of expert opinion as to the human duty involved in a vocation, calling, occupation, or employment."[2] This set of nonlegal rules or guidelines is ever evolving. Rupert Evans has noted that a code of ethics "is not static; it must be modified frequently to keep it in accord with the technology and with changing standards of society and of the profession."[3]

Since professional ethics relate to and come from the professional setting, it is appropriate to analyze them through hypothetical case studies that represent critical issues faced by industrial educators. Industrial education teachers find themselves increasingly confronted with critical decisions that require both legal and ethical consideration. Every day, they must make critical decisions related to students, colleagues, the community, administrators, equipment, materials, and money.

The following hypothetical case studies exemplify the critical decisions industrial educators face. After each case study, we offer questions to consider and suggested practices that help identify the ethical dimensions involved in the situation described. The use of these questions and practices in similar situations can help provide a basis for legal and ethical decision making.

Ethics Case Studies in Industrial Education

Use of Facilities

A common ethical issue confronting many industrial educators involves the use of facilities and equipment for purposes not related to instruction. Users of the facility and equipment might be another teacher, an administrator, janitor, or member of the community.

In the first case study, an assistant principal wants to use your industrial education facility with or without your permission to build a piece of furniture for use at home. What should you do? What are the ethical considerations?

Questions to Consider

1. Does the school or school district have a policy for faculty or staff use of school facilities? If so, what is your responsibility for enforcement?

2. Has the assistant principal received training in the proper and safe use of your equipment and facilities? Who determines what constitutes proper training and whether supervision is required?

3. Will the assistant principal pay for the project materials?

4. Who is responsible for any injury or equipment damage that might occur?

Suggested Practices

1. Make decisions about the use of facilities, tools, and equipment based on the relationship of the proposed activity to your program's

educational objectives and in compliance with your school's policy.

2. Any proposed use of facilities, tools, or equipment, other than for instruction, should be approved by the appropriate administrator.

3. Have a plan for supervision and safety instruction for any individual who uses your facilities, tools, or equipment.

Gifts and Conflict of Interest

In the course of interacting with business and industry in purchasing equipment and placing students, industrial educators may be offered incentives or special benefits from business or industry representatives.

In this case study, the owner of a local welding company offers you an expensive gift and thanks you profusely for recommending one of your best students.

Questions to Consider

1. Does your state or school district have a policy for gifts and potential conflict of interest? For example, the state of Oregon publishes an *Ethics Guide for Public Officials*. The code of ethics contained in this publication prevents any public state official from "soliciting or receiving calendar-year gifts with an aggregate value of over $100 from a source that has a legislative or administrative interest in [his or her] office."[4] Many school districts, colleges, or universities have established similar guidelines or policies for potential conflict of interest.

2. Did you follow appropriate procedures in recommending the student for employment? (See Chapter 5 for more information on recommendations.)

3. Were you solicitous in your actions, inviting the offer of a gift?

4. Did you consider asking the owner of the welding company to make an educational donation or contribution to your program that will benefit future students?

Suggested Practices

1. Identify the policies that apply to conflict of interest in receiving

gifts in your school, college, or state and make sure you comply with them.

2. Follow appropriate procedures in recommending students for employment and in purchasing equipment and supplies.

3. When gifts or donations are offered, suggest items that would improve your industrial education program.

Confidentiality

Industrial educators have access to confidential information in the course of their work. Such information may include academic records, personal or health information, and employment history.

In this case study, an industrial education teacher jokes about a student's academic and behavior problems with a group of neighbors.

Questions to Consider

As noted in our chapter on recommendations (Chapter 5), there is federal legislation regarding the confidentiality of student records. In addition, where the law leaves off, professional ethics and behavior begin. The actions of the industrial educator in the case study described above violate our Constitution's protection of an individual's privacy from governmental action.

1. Do you have a professional reason to discuss the student's academic and behavior problems with others?

2. Have you violated the student's privacy?

Suggested Practices

1. Consider confidential all student records and conversations with students, faculty, and parents, except where someone has a professional need to know certain information or in a situation that involves a serious question of health and safety.

2. Take steps to insure that students' academic achievements are not viewed or known by others.

3. Refrain from comparing students, especially siblings, outside the context of a professional relationship.

4. Discourage the disclosure of irrelevant and inappropriate information about the private lives of students or colleagues.

Equal Opportunity

Industrial educators develop and implement curricular programs that help students to learn about industry and technology and to prepare for jobs. Decisions and judgments made by industrial educators can have significant impact on their students' future.

Consider a case study in which an industrial educator fails to introduce a class composed primarily of minority students to the use of computers because the teacher assumes that the students will not use computers in future careers.

Questions to Consider

All laws that prohibit discrimination and provide for equal opportunity derive directly from the Constitution. The actual practice and enforcement of equal opportunity involves great subtlety and requires an individual ethical and moral commitment on the part of educators.

1. Do you have the same expectations of academic achievement and standards of personal conduct for all students regardless of their ethnic or cultural background?

2. Do you label and compare groups of students regarding classroom behavior, attitudes, and accomplishments?

3. Do you integrate your industrial education facility, using displays, assignments, and lectures that show people of different cultures in various roles?

Suggested Practices

1. Expect the same academic achievement and standards of personal conduct from all students, regardless of their ethnic background or cultural traditions.

2. Through the development and implementation of your curriculum, strive to provide equal opportunities for all students.

3. Avoid comparing or ranking groups of students with respect to behavior, attitudes, and accomplishments.

4. Avoid telling ethnic or cultural jokes. Also, discourage their telling by other teachers and students.

5. Encourage students to explore their cultural heritage through industrial education projects and activities.

Professionalism

Individual industrial educators represent their profession as a whole, and the profession represents each industrial educator. The actions of industrial educators define the image and perception of industrial education in the minds of students, parents, administrators, and the general public. Baker and Erickson emphasize the importance of "professional integrity, including such concepts as self-standards, self-commitment, continuation of the profession, and the advancement of the profession."[5]

In this case study, an industrial education teacher consistently uses poor grammar, spelling, and communication skills. The same teacher also dresses in a sloppy manner and uses foul language with students and parents.

Questions to Consider

1. Does this industrial educator consider the long-range impact of his or her actions?

2. Consider the message this sends to students. Using poor grammar or spelling tells your students that basic skills have little importance in industrial education.

Suggested Practices

1. Maintain a professional appearance through your dress and communications. Remember that you serve as a representative of your profession and a role model for your students.

2. All industrial educators should belong to representative local, state, and national associations. In addition to membership in these groups, industrial educators should contribute to the well-being of their profession.

3. Strive for continued personal and professional growth throughout your career.

4. Work with colleagues toward common goals and the betterment of industrial education and the overall education profession.

Education and a Code of Ethics

One indicator of a profession is an accepted code of ethics. The Hippocratic oath taken by medical doctors represents one well-known example of a professional code of ethics. Similar codes exist for lawyers, dentists, and engineers. Indeed, many educators believe that the lack of an accepted and recognized code of ethics stands in the way of the advancement of education as a profession. Ernest Boyer, president of the Carnegie Foundation for the Advancement of Teaching, has been quoted as saying, "Although such rituals may be mainly symbolic, they do represent one of the important ways a profession communicates to its new members and the public that there are high standards of ethics and personal behavior for which it stands."[6]

On the other hand, Daniel Callahan, in his article "Should There Be a Code of Ethics?" disagrees with Boyer, stating "My reservations [about a code of ethics] stem from two sources. The first source is my perception that codes of ethics have rarely, if ever, been adequate devices for dealing with the ethical problems of other fields or disciplines. No one today could confidently assert that the Code of Hippocrates is the salvation of the medical profession or that journalism has been notably improved because of codes drawn up by some professional organization."[7]

While the education profession does not have a single universally accepted code of ethics, there are several examples. We will review four: one for vocational educators, two for elementary and secondary teachers, and one for university and college professors. These examples of codes of ethics provide a reference and framework for the development of a code of ethics for industrial educators and offer a basis for critical decision making.

A Code of Ethics for Vocational Educators

The following code of ethics was adopted by the American Vocational Association delegate assembly in December 1979. The AVA is a professional association that represents administrators and teachers in agriculture, business, employment and training, health occupations, home economics, industrial arts, marketing, technical education, and trade and industrial education. Although not all industrial educators belong to the American Vocational Association, its code of ethics is an important reference.

The AVA Code of Ethics

The vocational educator believes in the worth and dignity of each individual and in the value of vocational education in enhancing individual development. Consequently, the vocational educator strives for the highest ethical standards to merit the respect and confidence of students, colleagues, and the community. They use their skills and knowledge to develop each of their students or colleagues to maximize human potential. This statement of *A Code of Ethics* provides a framework by which to guide vocational educators and the institutions through which they work in attaining the highest degree of professionalism.

With Respect to Self

The vocational educator:

- Represents personal and professional qualifications in a true and accurate manner.
- Maintains confidentiality of students and colleagues except where disclosure is compelled by law or to serve a compelling professional need.
- Bases professional action and decisions upon sound, objective rationale without influence of favors, gifts, or personal or political advantage.
- Recognizes and accepts responsibility for individual actions, judgments, and decisions.
- Strives throughout one's career to master, maintain, and improve professional competence through study, work, travel, and exploration.
- Contributes to growing body of specialized knowledge, concepts, and skills which characterize vocational education.
- Strives for the advancement of vocational education, upholds its honor and dignity, and works to strengthen it in the community, state, and nation.
- Participates actively in the work of professional organizations to define and improve standards of vocational education preparation and service.
- Establishes and maintains conditions of employment

conducive to providing high-quality vocational education.

● Performs one's duty as a teacher on the basis of careful preparation so instruction is accurate, current, objective, and scholarly, designed, to enhance the student's individual capabilities.

● Exercises professional judgment in presenting, interpreting, and critiquing ideas, including controversial issues.

● Joins with other professionals whose mission is to improve the delivery of vocational education to the nation's citizens.

With Respect to Others

● Uses individual competence as a principal criterion in accepting delegated responsibilities and assigning duties to others.

● Provides statements about a colleague or student in a fair, objective manner without embarrassment or ridicule.

● Provides educational and/or career options to all students or colleagues.

● Evaluates students and colleagues without regard to race, color, creed, sex, status, or any other factor unrelated to need for vocational education,

    a. allows any student or colleague to participate in the program who can benefit from the program.

    b. provides the same benefits or advantages to all students or colleagues in the program.

● Respects the rights and reputation of the student, colleague with whom one works, and the institution or organization with which one is affiliated.

● Acts to safeguard the health and safety of students and colleagues against incompetent, unethical, or illegal behavior of any person, whether student or colleague.

● Protects vocational education by promoting admission to the profession of persons who are fully qualified because of character, education, and experience, according to legally established criteria and standards.

● Promotes improvement of legalities affecting vocational education.

● Exercises professional judgment in the choice of teaching methods and materials appropriate to the needs and interests of each student.

● Influences effectively the formation of policies and procedures which affect one's professional work.

A Code of Ethics for Classroom Teachers

The following code of ethics was developed by the faculty of the College of Education at Michigan State University and presented by Judith Lanier and Philip Cusick in the June 1985 *Phi Delta Kappan.*

Code of Ethics for Classroom Teachers

I hereby affirm my dedication to the profession of education. With this affirmation, I embrace the obligations of professional educators to improve the general welfare, to advance human understanding and competence, and to bring honor to the endeavors of teaching and learning. I accept these obligations for myself and will be vigilant and responsibile in supporting their acceptance by my colleagues.

I will be always mindful of my responsibility to increase the intelligence of students through the disciplined pursuit of knowledge. I will be steadfast in this commitment, even when weary and tempted to abdicate such responsibility or blame failure on obstacles that make the task difficult. I will be persistent in my commitment to foster respect for a life of learning and respect for all students.

To perform faithfully these professional duties, I promise to work always to better understand my content, my instructional practice, and the students who come under my tutelage. I promise to seek and support policies that promote quality in teaching and learning and to provide all engaged in education the opportunity to achieve excellence. I promise to emulate personally the qualities I wish to foster, and to hold and forever honor a democratic way of life that cannot exist without disciplined, cultivated, and free minds.

I recognize that at times my endeavors will offend privilege and status, that I will be opposed by bias and defenders of inequality, and that I will have to confront arguments that seek to discourage my efforts and diminish my hope. But I will remain faithful to the belief that these endeavors and the pursuit of these goals make me worthy of my profession, and my profession worthy of a free people.

Lanier and Cusick note four critical elements in the oath: (1) dedication to the profession of education, (2) dedication to students, (3) the concept of an educator as a lifelong learner, and (4) dedication to equal opportunity through education.[8]

The National Education Association (NEA) representative assembly adopted the following code of ethics in July 1975.

NEA Code of Ethics for the Education Profession

Principle I: Commitment to the Student

The educator strives to help each student realize his or her potential as a worthy and effective member of society. The educator therefore works to stimulate the spirit of inquiry, the acquisition of knowledge and understanding, and the thoughtful formulation of worthy goals.

In fulfillment of the obligation to the student, the educator:

1. Shall not unreasonably restrain the student from independent action in the pursuit of learning.

2. Shall not unreasonably deny the student access to varying points of view.

3. Shall not deliberately suppress or distort subject matter relevant to the student's progress.

4. Shall make reasonable effort to protect the student from conditions harmful to learning or to health and safety.

5. Shall not intentionally expose the student to embarrassment or disparagement.

6. Shall not on the basis of race, color, creed, sex, national origin, marital status, political or religious beliefs, family, social or cultural background, or sexual orientation unfairly:

   a. Exclude any student from participation in any program;

   b. Deny benefits to any student;

   c. Grant any advantage to any student.

7. Shall not use professional relationships with students for private advantage.

8. Shall not disclose information about students obtained in the course of professional service, unless disclosure serves a compelling professional purpose or is required by law.

Principle II: Commitment to the Profession

The education profession is vested by the public with a trust and responsibility requiring the highest ideals of professional service.

In the belief that the quality of the services of the education profession directly influences the nation and its citizens, the educator shall exert every effort to raise professional standards, to promote a climate that encourages the exercise of professional judgment to achieve conditions which attract persons worthy of the trust to careers in education, and to assist in preventing the practice of the profession by unqualified persons.

In fulfillment of the obligation to the profession, the educator:

1. Shall not in an application for a professional position deliberately make a false statement or fail to disclose a material fact related to competency and qualifications.

2. Shall not misrepresent his/her professional qualifications.

3. Shall not assist entry into the profession of a person known to be unqualified in respect to character, education, or other relevant attribute.

4. Shall not knowingly make a false statement concerning the qualifications of a candidate for a professional position.

5. Shall not assist a non-educator in the unauthorized practice of teaching.

6. Shall not disclose information about colleagues obtained in the course of professional service unless disclosure serves a compelling professional purpose or is required by law.

7. Shall not knowingly make false or malicious statements about a colleague.

8. Shall not accept any gratuity, gift, or favor that might impair or appear to influence professional decisions or actions.

A Code of Ethics for Administrators

The following statement of ethics was adopted by the American Association of School Administrators Executive Committee in May 1981.

Statement of Ethics for School Administrators

The educational administrator:

1. Makes the well-being of students the fundamental value of all decision making and actions.

2. Fulfills professional responsibilities with honesty and integrity.

3. Supports the principle of due process and protects the civil and human rights of all individuals.

4. Obeys local, state, and national laws and does not knowingly join or support organizations that advocate, directly or indirectly, the overthrow of the government.

5. Implements the governing board of education's policies and administrative rules and regulations.

6. Pursues appropriate measures to correct those laws, policies, and regulations that are not consistent with sound educational goals.

7. Avoids using positions for personal gain through political, social, religious, economic, or other influence.

8. Accepts academic degrees or professional certification only from duly accredited institutions.

9. Maintains the standards and seeks to improve the effectiveness of the profession through research and continuing professional development.

10. Honors all contracts until fulfillment, release, or dissolution mutually agreed upon by all parties to contract.

A Code of Ethics for University Professors

The following is excerpted from the 1966 American Association of University Professors statement of professional ethics.

1. The professor, guided by a deep conviction of the worth and dignity of the advancement of knowledge, recognizes the special responsibilities placed upon [him or her] . . . to seek and to state the truth as [he or she] sees it.

2. As a teacher, the professor encourages the. . .pursuit of learning in [his or her] students.

3. As a colleague, the professor has obligations that derive from common membership in the community of scholars.

Implications for Industrial Educators

Industrial educators do not have a formal accepted code of ethics. Rupert Evans called for the development of one when he identified as prerequisites for professionalism "a code of ethics to which the professionals are expected to adhere, and means for judging and expelling those who violate it most flagrantly."[9] Along with the AVA's code of ethics, the existing codes of ethics for teachers, administrators, professors, and the case studies in this chapter can assist industrial educators in making critical decisions.

In summary, use the following as guidelines in analyzing and making critical decisions:

1. Relate your decisions and actions to the central purpose of helping students learn and grow.

2. As you work with students, try to give each one equal opportunities in his or her educational program.

3. Seek the advice and counsel of colleagues, administrators, and your professional associations.

4. Dedicate yourself to bettering the profession of industrial education through your actions and contributions.

References

[1] *Webster's Ninth New Collegiate Dictionary.* Springfield, Mass.: Merriam-Webster, Inc., 1986, 426, 427.

[2] Gauerke, W. E., *Legal and Ethical Responsibilities of School Personel.* Englewood Cliffs, N.J.: Prentice-Hall, 1959, 17.

[3] Evans, R. E. "The Professionalism of AVA: Are We Running a Loose Ship?" *American Vocational Association Journal* 47 (1972), no. 7, 22-23.

[4] Oregon Government Ethics Commission. *Ethics Guide for Public Officials.* Salem, Oreg.: Oregon Government Ethics Commission, 1985.

[5] Baker, G., and D. Erickson. "A Perspective on Professionalism." *Man, Society, Technology* 42 (1983), no. 4, 2.

[6]Lanier, J., and P. Cusik. "An Oath for Professional Educators." *Phi Delta Kappan* 66 (1985), no. 10, 711-12.

[7]Callahan, D. "Should There Be an Academic Code of Ethics?" *Journal of Higher Education* 53 (1982), no. 3, 335-44.

[8]Lanier, J., and P. Cusick, op., cit.

[9]Evans, op. cit.

Resources

Kimbrough, R. B. *Ethics: A Course of Study for Educational Leaders.* Arlington, Va.: The American Association of School Administrators, 1985.

National Education Association. *Code of Ethics of the Education Profession.* Washington, D.C.: National Education Association, 1975.

Robertson, E., and G. Grant. "Teaching and Ethics: An Epilogue." *Journal of Higher Education* 53 (1982), no. 3, 345-57.

Shurr, G. M. "Toward a Code of Ethics for Academics." *Journal of Higher Education* 53 (1982) no. 3, 318-34.

Index